Walth~~ ~

A CENTURY OF REMEMBRANCE

One Hundred Outstanding British War Memorials

DEREK BOORMAN

Pen & Sword
MILITARY

First published in Great Britain by
PEN & SWORD MILITARY
an imprint of
Pen & Sword Books Limited
47 Church Street, Barnsley
S. Yorkshire, S70 2AS

Copyright © Derek Boorman, 2005

ISBN 1 84415 316 9

The right of Derek Boorman to be
identified as Author of this Work has
been asserted by him in accordance with
the Copyright, Designs and Patents Act 1988.

Except where otherwise stated,
recent photographs were taken by the author.

A CIP catalogue record for this book
is available from the British Library.

Designed and typeset (in 10pt Sabon)
by Sylvia Menzies, Pen & Sword Books Ltd

Printed and bound in Great Britain by
CPI UK

Pen & Sword Books Ltd incorporates the imprints of
Pen & Sword Aviation, Pen & Sword Maritime, Pen & Sword Military,
Wharncliffe Local History, Pen & Sword Select,
Pen & Sword Military Classics and Leo Cooper.

For a complete list of Pen & Sword titles please contact:
PEN & SWORD BOOKS LIMITED
47 Church Street, Barnsley, South Yorkshire, S70 2AS, England.
E-mail: enquiries@pen-and-sword.co.uk
Website: www.pen-and-sword.co.uk

ONTENTS

FOREWORD
by
W.F. Deedes

We have never fully understood what those two World Wars cost us. It was not the treasure we lost nor the debts we incurred that counted. It was the blood we lost, particularly in The Great War. We grievously depleted our stock. Our war memorials stand as a valuable reminder of this truth. Most of them, as Derek Boorman's book testifies, were erected after the First World War when dying for your country was deeply respected, men doffed the hats they then wore when they passed the Cenotaph in Whitehall, and on Armistice Day many sang 'O valiant hearts...' in tears. If you go to see the huge memorials in the battlefields of France, raised to those who died in the First World War, or even to see the mercifully smaller ones of the Second World War, you do understand what those victories cost us. But many never go that way. The only evidence of what was sacrificed are our local war memorials. When you see in a still small village a memorial with a dozen names on it, then you draw close to the truth.

As one whose childhood was darkened by the First World War and who took part in the Second World War, I dimly realise in my old age how many of today's difficulties and failings are attributable to those wars. They were a turning point in our history. That is why these memorials must stand in good repair, a reminder to later, more forgetful and careless generations of the human cost of total war.

$\mathscr{A}$CKNOWLEDGEMENTS

I wish particularly to pay tribute to the late Sir Donald Thompson, former Director General of the War Memorials Trust, whose quiet persuasion prompted the writing of this book to assist his beloved charity.

Jane Furlong of the National Inventory of War Memorials has been extremely helpful and generous with her time, and it is heartening to see the great progress that has been made and is still being made at the Inventory.

As ever, I should like to thank my wife Rena for her encouragement and assistance, and Barbara Jones for the hours spent on correspondence and administration.

Finally, I wish to acknowledge the following sources of information, Accrington Library, H. Barratt, Belfast City Council, T. Berry, Blackburn Library, A. Borg (*War Memorials*), Burnley Library, E. Challinor, K. Collen, Commonwealth War Graves Commission, Dornock Library, C. Duckworth, Maj. J.M. Dunlop, S. Elliott, L. Eyre, Fermanagh District Council, D. Ferne, A. Firth, B. Fisher, J. Gildea (*For Remembrance*), Greenock Central Library, S. Halstead, C. Harman, Harrow School, D. Hindmarch, J. Hockey, J. Justice, D. Leeman, R.J. McBrayne, Col. R. McCrum, R. Maclean, J. Morrison, National Memorial Arboretum, Oldham Archives, Paisley Central Library, Pangbourne College, Portsmouth Cathedral, Rolls Royce, L. Rowley, Royal Inniskilling Fusiliers Regimental Museum, Royston Library, Rugby School, St. Anne's Library, Sheffield Central Library, Stockport Art Gallery, Stonehaven Library, M. Sumner, Thornton Library, Rev. Dr. M.E. Weymont, Wirral Archives.

Brigade of Guards Memorial, Crimean War.

$\mathcal{I}$NTRODUCTION

A Century of Remembrance is a study of 100 outstanding United Kingdom war memorials which commemorate twentieth century conflicts from the Boer War to the Falklands and Gulf wars. The first described is a Boer War memorial unveiled on 5 November 1904, and the last is the Animals in War memorial unveiled in London on 24 November 2004.

The memorials chosen are listed as near as possible in chronological order, although in a few cases evidence of the actual unveiling or dedication date is vague. The choice of the one hundred was determined by several factors, but principally, the need to represent a number of different wars, a number of different artists and a variety of types of memorial in form and in purpose. A geographical element also came into the consideration.

Obviously there are also interesting war memorials to those who died in conflicts before the twentieth century. An outstanding example is that to the Brigade of Guards dead of the Crimean War, standing in Waterloo Place, London, with guardsmen figures cast from captured Russian guns.

However, almost all of our country's war memorials are since 1900. After the Boer War in which nearly 6,000 British soldiers died and almost 23,000 were wounded, the number of memorials dedicated was almost 1,000. This was a significant figure which was, of course, dwarfed by the huge numbers following the First World War to commemorate the million dead of Britain and the Empire. After the Second World War with almost half a million British combatants and some 70,000 civilians dead, fewer new memorials were built as in many cases the memorials to the Great War were adapted to recognise the later dead.

Nevertheless, some of our finest memorials are to the Second World War and, in addition, we have memorials to the Spanish Civil War, to Korea, to the Falklands, to the Gulf, and to those killed in smaller conflicts and in Northern Ireland.

It is necessary to limit fuller consideration of some sculptors and architects due to their prodigious output. An obvious example is Sir Edwin Lutyens who designed the Cenotaph in Whitehall and so many other war memorials that in a study of only one hundred works it is difficult to do full justice to him. There are many others in this category.

An attempt has been made to include most different types of memorial from statues and stained glass windows to arches, obelisks and cenotaphs, and from chapels and cloisters to art galleries and gardens and even a carillon.

Categories from individual to national memorials are represented and

The Cenotaph in Whitehall, described by The Times, *as 'simple', 'massive', 'unadorned', was designed by Sir Edward Lutyens for the Victory Parade on 19 July 1919. It commemorates the British Dead of both World Wars and subsequent wars.*

Animals in War memorial, unveiled on 24 November 2004 at Brook Gate, Park Lane, London, by the Princess Royal.

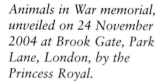

include memorials in schools, churches and places of work, and those representing communities and the armed services.

It would not be difficult to base a war memorial study on London alone but again, geographically, the memorials chosen are spread more widely although inevitably, some areas are better represented than others.

In recent years the need to maintain and preserve our war memorials has become increasingly recognised. The excellent work of the National Inventory of War Memorials, originally funded by the Leverhulme Trust and managed jointly by the Imperial War Museum and the Royal Commission on the Historical Monuments of England, has added greatly to our knowledge and appreciation. Inaugurated in 1989 the Inventory is in the process of establishing independent charity status. It has details already of some 53,000 UK memorials out of an estimated total of 60,000 (although the estimate has already been amended upwards more than once) and plans eventually to have a database complete with images of the memorials and records of the estimated 1.5 million names on the memorials. An appeal was launched by the Inventory in February 2005 to raise over £2 million to complete this vast project.

Another organisation, the War Memorials Trust, formerly Friends of War Memorials, was registered in 1997, and a recent quarterly bulletin listed its objectives as, in its own words,

1. To monitor the condition of War Memorials and to take steps to ensure that local authorities and other relevant organisations are alerted to such condition with a view to their undertaking any necessary restoration, essential maintenance, repairs and cleaning.

2. To liaise with secular and ecclesiastical authorities, regiments and other responsible bodies with a view to their accepting responsibility for, and undertaking repairs to and restoration of War Memorials.

3. To publicise and to educate and inform the public about the spiritual, archaeological, artistic, aesthetic and historical significance of War Memorials as part of our national heritage; to encourage support groups and to inspire young people to cherish their local War Memorials and the memory of those who sacrificed their lives in the cause of freedom.

Grants from the Trust and from English Heritage are available for small restoration projects but existing funds are far short of the sums required to meet all requests.

With this in mind, the royalties from the sale of *A Century of Remembrance* will be donated to the War Memorials Trust. In addition, donations will be made to the Animals in War Memorial Fund.

$\mathcal{H}$ULL

The war memorial in Paragon Square, Hull, is unusual in that it commemorates the city's dead of all wars, from the Boer War onwards. The original memorial is a stone statue of two soldiers in Boer War khaki, one with rifle in hand standing over his wounded companion who is handing the other his last cartridge. The work is on a rough granite base, in turn on a plinth bearing a brass plate, with the inscription,

ERECTED BY PUBLIC SUBSCRIPTION TO THE
MEMORY OF THE MEN OF HULL WHO LOST
THEIR LIVES DURING THE SOUTH AFRICAN WAR
1899, 1900, 1901 AND 1902.

Other plates list the dead as eight killed in action, four died of wounds, and the incredibly high number of forty-five died of 'disease etc.'.

The memorial was unveiled by the Mayor, Alderman Williams, on 5 November 1904.

Twenty years later, on 20 September 1924, to the rear of the South African War memorial, Hull's Great War Cenotaph was unveiled by Field Marshal Sir William Robertson, after a war in which 70,000, out of a population of 290,000, answered the call for men.

On the stone of the later memorial are now the words,

ERECTED TO THE MEMORY OF THE MEN OF
KINGSTON-UPON-HULL WHO LAID DOWN THEIR
LIVES FOR THEIR COUNTRY IN THE GREAT WAR 1914-1918
AND THE WORLD WAR 1939-1945
THEIR NAME LIVETH FOR EVERMORE.

Lower down has been added,

AND IN MEMORY OF THOSE WHO GAVE THEIR LIVES
IN LATER CONFLICTS.

Nearby are marble slabs commemorating the Korean War (1950-53), and four Hull recipients of the Victoria Cross.

Another interesting feature is a replica of a post marking the extent of the German advance in 1914–18, such posts being common in France and Belgium. This post was presented to Hull by the people of Oppy in France, where there is a Somme battlefield memorial to the men of Hull.

KING'S LIVERPOOL REGIMENT

The memorial erected in St John's Gardens, Liverpool to commemorate the Boer War, and earlier, dead of the King's Liverpool Regiment, was unveiled on 9 September 1905 by Field Marshal Sir George White VC. It was designed by W. Goscombe John who, after the First World War, was responsible for some of the very finest memorials, at Port Sunlight, in Newcastle and at Llandaff.

A granite pedestal and central column support bronze figures of Britannia, of a soldier of 1685, and of a Boer War soldier, while at the rear is a bronze seated drummer boy of Marlborough's army.

The pedestal is decorated by military equipment, wreaths, palms and a Union Jack, and inscribed battle honours of,

> BLENHEIM, RAMILLIES, OUDENARDE, MALPLAQUET, DETTINGEN, MARTINIQUE, NIAGARA, DELHI, LUCKNOW, PEIWAR, KOTAL, DEFENCE OF LADYSMITH.

On the front is inscribed,

> THIS MONUMENT IS ERECTED BY THE OFFICERS, NON-COMMISSIONED OFFICERS, AND MEN OF THE REGIMENT, AIDED BY THE GRATEFUL CONTRIBUTIONS OF THE PEOPLE OF LIVERPOOL, IN MEMORY OF THEIR COMRADES AND FELLOW CITIZENS WHO DIED DURING THE CAMPAIGN IN AFGHANISTAN 1878-1880, BURMAH 1885–1887, AND SOUTH AFRICA 1899–1902.
> SOME FELL ON THE FIELD OF BATTLE, SOME DIED OF WOUNDS, AND SOME OF DISEASE, BUT ALL GAVE THEIR LIVES FOR THE HONOUR OF THEIR REGIMENT, THEIR CITY AND THEIR COUNTRY. PRO PATRIA.

In all, 66 deaths are recorded in the Afghanistan campaign, 110 in Burmah and 173 in South Africa.

This wonderful memorial, typical of the work of Goscombe John, is unfortunately in need of some restoration. The inscriptions to the front are badly worn, the flag is damaged and there is a certain amount of graffiti on the stonework.

ROYAL SCOTS GREYS

The Edinburgh Boer War Memorial to the 2nd Dragoons, the Royal Scots Greys, is on the south side of Princes Street, at pavement level, and has the dramatic background of the castle and its rock. Sculpted by Birnie Rhind of Edinburgh, the memorial is a twelve foot high bronze equestrian statue of a trooper of the Greys on a massive rock pedestal and it was unveiled by the Earl of Rosebery on 16 November 1906.

The original bronze inscription panel on the Princes Street side of the pedestal is decorated at each top corner by a French eagle, the badge of the regiment since Waterloo.

Above the names of seven officers and sixty-nine NCOs and men is the inscription,

IN MEMORY OF OFFICERS, NON-COMMISSIONED OFFICERS
AND MEN THE ROYAL SCOTS GREYS WHO GAVE THEIR
LIVES FOR THEIR COUNTRY IN THE BOER WAR 1899–1902.

The names of the dead are listed in order of rank, as they are on subsequent panels commemorating the First and Second World Wars.

On the original panel one man is listed as 'TRUMPETER' and two as 'SHOEING SMITHS'.

$\mathscr{B}$LACK WATCH

On The Mound in Edinburgh, overlooking Princes Street, is the imposing Boer War Memorial to the Black Watch Regiment. Situated on a corner near the Bank of Scotland building, the memorial is a bronze statue of a Highlander measuring 11 foot 6 inches in height on a granite pedestal 16 foot high.

On the front of the pedestal is the inscription,

TO THE MEMORY OF THE OFFICERS, NON-COMMISSIONED
OFFICERS AND MEN OF THE BLACK WATCH WHO FELL IN
THE SOUTH AFRICAN WAR 1899–1902.

Also on the front, and above the inscription, is a bronze battle scene of the regiment being piped into the attack.

Bronze inscription panels on the sides of the pedestal list those of the regiment who died during the war, in total fifteen officers and 198 men, including a major-general and a lieutenant-colonel.

Interestingly, one panel lists those who died in action or of wounds, while the other lists those who died of disease during the war, with some forty per cent falling into the latter category.

The memorial was the work of Birnie Rhind, the Edinburgh sculptor, and was accepted by Edinburgh's Lord Provost on 27 June 1910.

IMPERIAL CAMEL CORPS

The 1920 memorial to the First World War dead of the Imperial Camel Corps is in the Victoria Embankment Gardens, London. These gardens have a wealth of memorials, a large number of which are related to the two world wars, and the Camel Corps Memorial, although one of the smallest, is one of the most interesting and attractive.

A bronze figure of a soldier mounted on a camel is supported by a stone pedestal on the sides of which are two bronze relief plaques of men in action, and two bronze name tablets. One of the name plates lists men of the British, New Zealand and Indian contingents, while the other is dedicated to the Australian contingent alone.

An inscription reads,

TO THE GLORIOUS AND IMMORTAL
MEMORY OF THE OFFICERS, N.C.O.'S
AND MEN OF THE IMPERIAL CAMEL
CORPS, BRITISH, AUSTRALIAN, NEW
ZEALAND AND INDIAN, WHO FELL IN
ACTION OR DIED OF WOUNDS AND
DISEASE IN EGYPT, SINAI AND
PALESTINE. 1916–1917–1918.

Another inscription lists the Corps' engagements by year, seven engagements in 1916, eight in 1917, and three in 1918.

The memorial sculptor was Cecil Brown and the bronzes were cast, as were many at that time, by A.B. Burton of Thames Ditton.

EDITH CAVELL

The memorial to Nurse Edith Cavell is in St Martin's Place, London, near the National Portrait Gallery and looking towards Trafalgar Square.

At dawn on 12 October 1915 she was executed by the Germans in Brussels for harbouring and assisting allied soldiers. At the court martial she admitted having helped 60 British and French soldiers and about 100 French and Belgian men of military age to escape to Holland. She had been matron of Berkendael Medical Institute in Brussels, later a Red Cross Hospital.

The execution caused particular revulsion in Britain at the time, and the crowd at the unveiling of her memorial by Queen Alexandra in 1920 was even more than usually emotional.

The monument by Sir George Frampton did not escape artistic criticism. The heavy plinth supports a cross with figures of a woman and child, 'Humanity Protecting the Small States', and the inscription FOR KING AND COUNTRY.

At a lower level is a stone statue of Edith Cavell, in matron's uniform, and under it is carved, EDITH CAVELL. BRUSSELS. DAWN OCTOBER 12TH 1915.

Inscribed on the sides of the monument are the words, HUMANITY, SACRIFICE, FORTITUDE and DEVOTION.

Edith Cavell's own words, PATRIOTISM IS NOT ENOUGH. I MUST HAVE NO HATRED OR BITTERNESS FOR ANYONE were added several years after the unveiling, and inscribed below the date of her execution.

FOR
KING
AND
COUNTRY

HUMANITY

BRUSSELS
DAWN
OCTOBER 12TH
1915

EDITH CAVELL
BRUSSELS
DAWN
OCTOBER 12TH
1915
PATRIOTISM IS NOT ENOUGH
I MUST HAVE NO HATRED OR
BITTERNESS FOR ANYONE

WAGGONERS

Sir Mark Sykes of Sledmere, local landowner and MP for Central Hull, served during the First World War as commander of the 5th Yorkshires, until being moved to staff duties. He died suddenly in February 1919 when in attendance at the Paris Peace Conference and he is one of the men commemorated on the panels of the Queen Eleanor Cross at Sledmere.

Nearby is a unique Great War memorial for which he was responsible, although he did not live to see its dedication.

The memorial is twenty foot high, of Portland stone, and is cylindrical in shape on a stepped base with four columns and carved reliefs. Round the top is the inscription,

> LT. COL. SIR MARK SYKES BART. M.P. DESIGNED THIS
> MONUMENT AND SET IT UP AS A REMEMBRANCE
> OF THE GALLANT SERVICES RENDERED IN THE
> GREAT WAR 1914–1919 BY THE WAGGONERS
> RESERVE A CORPS OF 1000 DRIVERS RAISED BY HIM
> ON THE YORKSHIRE WOLD FARMS IN THE YEAR 1912.

This group of skilled men from the Wolds was not only raised but also trained by him, in fields close to the site of the memorial. They went to France early in the war and casualties were heavy. The monument is to both the fallen and the survivors and was erected by Lady Sykes, and unveiled in September 1920 by Lieutenant General Sir Ivor Maxse, C.-in-C. Northern Command.

Executed by sculptor Carlo Magnoni of London, and Albert Barr, the estate mason, the memorial has a series of carvings, in primitive style, depicting the activities of the Waggoners (to use the spelling of the inscription), from peace time to enlistment, from their farewells to their families to their landing in France, and from early scenes of action and of German atrocities, to the Waggoners driving the enemy back across the Marne.

The scenes depicting the Germans burning a church and executing a female civilian apparently led to complaints in the 1930s but a German embassy request for the removal of the monument was unsurprisingly not successful.

Regular reunions of the Waggoners were held over the years, with a final official reunion held on 7 August 1988 when the last of the group, five in number, were invited to be guests of honour at Sledmere House.

OUTHAMPTON

S outhampton's Cenotaph was designed by Sir Edwin Lutyens who was consulted by the city's war memorial committee as early as January 1919, and his eventual design for Southampton, with some modification, later became the basis for the design of the Cenotaph in Whitehall. His long list of memorial commissions eventually also included Manchester, Northampton, Leicester, Bury, Norwich, Southend, the Merchant Navy memorial at Tower Hill, the NER memorial in York and those at Wellington College and Thiepval on the Somme.

Lutyens' original brief was for a memorial at a cost not exceeding £10,000, and his first scheme, for a pair of archways to the entrances to East and West Park, proved to be too costly and was replaced by the present design and built on a site at the eastern entrance to West Park.

The memorial booklet describes the memorial as follows:

'Here, facing west is the Great War Stone of Remembrance, a monolith, an altar in form, identical to those which lie in each of our War Cemeteries throughout the War area, with the words chosen by Mr Rudyard Kipling – Their name liveth for evermore – cut on its west face. Behind this stone, on a plinth, standing on a platform of steps, rises a great pylon.

On the north, south and west faces of this pylon, recessed in panels, are inscribed the 1,800 names of those who fell in the Great War. The panels being recessed, and the stones that built them being on their natural bed, the inscription is permanent.

The east side, facing the main road, contains a Great Cross, and on its surface is carved a sword crosswise. On the plinth is carved a Wreath of Victory. The pylon is surmounted by a cenotaph, supported north and south by lions and east and west by the Arms of Southampton.

On the cenotaph is placed a recumbent effigy of a fighting man. In that the effigy is placed high up, the face is not to be seen, so that in the imagination it represents to every mother her son. The wreaths upon the cenotaph enclose emblems of the Army and Navy, including the Mercantile Marine, and Air Force, represented by the Anchor and the Royal Cypher.

Flanking the Monument are piers terminated with fir cones, emblems of eternity, joined by a wall and seat, and the words 'Our Glorious Dead' are inscribed on the wall.

The whole of the Memorial is built of specially selected Portland stone, the best stone in England for durability, and weathering to a beautiful colour, growing whiter with age and retaining the character of the design.'

The number of names inscribed on the memorial eventually increased to 2,008, as the committee continued to advertise for a further six months to make sure that no names were omitted, but unfortunately the engraving is now beginning to show signs of wear and although work has been done to combat this, further restoration will be required, a problem not peculiar to this memorial.

The unveiling ceremony was held on 6 November 1920, the unveiling being carried out by Lord Lieutenant Major-General Seeley and the dedication by the Bishop of Winchester, the Right Reverend Edward Stuart.

There are now two pedestals supporting stone books to the west of the Great War Stone. One is dedicated to the men, women and children of Southampton who lost their lives in the Second World War, and the other to all citizens of Southampton who have given their lives in the service of their country.

CLAYTON-LE-MOORS

The main feature of an attractive monument in a corner of Mercer Park in Clayton-le-Moors, is the group of two bronze figures, one a soldier with helmet and rifle and the other a robed female symbolising 'FAITH'. With one hand round his shoulder she appears with her other hand to be pointing out to him the path which duty dictates.

The square plinth of Portland stone originally carried bronze name panels which have since been replaced by slate.

To the original 225 names, including two VAD nurses, of the First World War, have been added twenty-eight 1939–45 names and one from the Korean War.

The original inscription to The Great War 1914–1919 has been amended to read,

> TO OUR GLORIOUS DEAD WHO FELL IN
> THE TWO WORLD WARS.

and other inscriptions are,

> THEIR NAME LIVETH FOR EVERMORE   and

> PASS NOT IN SORROW BUT IN LOWLY PRIDE AND
> STRIVE TO LIVE AS NOBLY AS THEY DIED.

The memorial was designed by John Cassidy, who was responsible also for memorials at Skipton and Stourbridge and it was unveiled on Saturday, 6 November 1920 by Major-General A. Solly-Flood, the former commander of the 42nd (East Lancashire) Division in which many local men served.

The 1939–1945 plaque was unveiled on 11 December 1949 by Mrs. A. Campbell who had lost two sons in the war.

THE CENOTAPH

The Cenotaph in Whitehall commemorates the British Dead of both World Wars and subsequent wars. Designed by Sir Edward Lutyens, it was originally made in plaster and wood for the Victory Parade on 19 July 1919 and it was only afterwards, in response to public demand, that it was reconstructed in its present form of Portland stone. Part of the original wooden structure was preserved at the Imperial War Museum until destroyed by a Second World War bomb.

The Times described the Cenotaph as 'simple, massive, unadorned', and its art critic spoke of 'the common sense of the design' and said 'Sir Edward Lutyens has not tried to pile up a collection of architectural features'.

Certainly, simplicity is the outstanding impression given by the huge, classical, stepped pylon at the top of which is the tomb, and there is an almost complete lack of decoration.

The monument was unveiled on Armistice Day, 11 November 1920, by King George V, who was accompanied by the Prince of Wales, the Duke of York, Prince Henry and the Duke of Connaught, all in uniform. On the stroke of 11 o'clock the King pressed the button to release the flag covering the Cenotaph, then followed the silence which was finally broken by the Last Post.

After the ceremony the procession moved to Westminster Abbey for the funeral of the Unknown Warrior. From the Cenotaph King George V walked immediately behind the coffin which was carried on a gun carriage of the Royal Horse Artillery, with a bearer party of Coldstream Guards. At the Abbey the twelve pall bearers included Lord Haig, Lord French and Lord Beatty, and 100 VCs formed a guard of honour.

In 1946 an additional inscription referring to the dead of the Second World War was unveiled by King George VI. An annual Service of Remembrance is, of course, still held to this day at the Cenotaph, and royal wreaths are still the first to be laid.

The Unknown Warrior.

The wreaths of the royal party.

EN OF LONDON

The principal inscription on the war memorial in front of the Royal Exchange reads,

> TO THE IMMORTAL HONOUR OF THE OFFICERS,
> NON-COMMISSIONED OFFICERS AND MEN OF LONDON
> WHO SERVED THEIR KING AND EMPIRE IN THE GREAT WAR
> 1914–1919. THIS MEMORIAL IS DEDICATED IN PROUD
> AND GRATEFUL RECOGNITION BY THE CITY
> AND COUNTY OF LONDON.

On the back of the memorial there is inscribed a list of London battalions, from those of the London Regiment to those of the Artillery, Yeomanry and Engineers.

The monument was designed by Sir Aston Webb with sculpture by Alfred Drury, and was unveiled on 12 November 1920 by the Duke of York.

The main stone column of the memorial is surmounted by the bronze figure of a lion supporting a shield with the figure of St George and the dragon in relief, while at the base are two fine bronze military statues holding rifles but at ease.

A further inscription since added is,

> AND ALBEIT MANY UNITS NAMED HEREON HAVE
> CHANGED IN DESIGNATION AND ROLE WE HONOUR
> AND REMEMBER THE MEN AND WOMEN WHO SERVED
> IN ALL THE UNITS OF THE CITY AND COUNTY OF
> LONDON IN THE WAR OF 1939–1945.

*H*UNTRISS BROTHERS

ithin the parish church of All Saints in the village of Mattersey, Nottinghamshire, is a memorial window to three sons of the Huntriss family who lived at Mattersey Hall at the time of the First World War. The 1920 window, by Kayll and Reed of Leeds, is divided into three, each part showing the figure of a medieval youth in armour either kneeling or looking upwards towards an image of Christ holding before him a crown.

At the top of the window are the words,

> BE THOU FAITHFUL UNTO DEATH AND I WILL GIVE
> THEE A CROWN OF LIFE.

while the inscription at the foot of the window reads,

> IN EVER LOVING MEMORY OF LIEUT. WILLIAM HUNTRISS,
> 3RD DUKE OF WELLINGTON'S WEST RIDING REGIMENT
> (ATTACHED TO GOLD COAST REGT.) BORN DECEMBER 16TH
> 1886. DIED OCTOBER 23RD 1918 AT COOMASSIE, AFRICA.

> CAPT. HAROLD EDWARDS HUNTRISS, 1ST BATTALION
> BEDFORDSHIRE REGIMENT. BORN MAY 23RD 1890. DIED OF
> WOUNDS AT FESTHUBERT, FRANCE, MAY 17TH 1915.

> CAPT. CYRIL JOHN HUNTRISS, 1ST BATTALION EAST
> YORKSHIRE REGIMENT. BORN JANUARY 29TH 1893. KILLED AT
> FRICOURT, FRANCE, JULY 1ST 1916. THE THREE SONS OF
> WILLIAM HUNTRISS, LATE OF MATTERSEY HALL, AND
> CHARLOTTE ELIZABETH, HIS WIFE.

> THE LORD GAVE AND THE LORD HATH TAKEN AWAY.

> BLESSED BE THE NAME OF THE LORD.

Mattersey Hall is now a Bible College but from 1947 until 1972 was a boys' preparatory school, and the custom on Remembrance Day was for each boy to place his poppy on the ledge under the Huntriss window at the end of the service in church.

The names of the Huntriss brothers, along with those of some four hundred others, are also commemorated on the walls of the Uppingham School Great War Memorial Chapel. William Huntriss Junior had been in the shooting team at Uppingham and gone on to become a solicitor; Harold Edwards Huntriss went on to the Royal Military College at

Sandhurst and was a regular soldier at the outbreak of war; and Cyril John Huntriss had a distinguished school career, being a school praeposter, and in the school rugby, hockey and running teams. In the war he won the Military Cross and was mentioned in Dispatches.

The Huntriss window in All Saints Church is still a beautiful and moving memorial and although some years ago it appeared to be endangered by the poor condition of the stonework in that part of the church, including that around the window, remedial work has since taken place.

Next to the window in the church is a tablet listing the nineteen men of the parish who died in 1914–18 to whom the tablet and a clock in the church tower were erected in 1921. Amongst the names are three Huntriss, two Darwin, two Glasby, two Smithson and two Taylor. There has been the addition of one name for the Second World War.

$\mathscr{K}$IRKCUDBRIGHT

he site of the Kirkcudbright war memorial is in front of medieval
Maclellan's Castle, and the massive bronze warrior of the memorial
is similarly from an age long before the Great War. The base of the
memorial is of rugged stones from the nearby seashore, carved with thistles
stretching from stone to stone. The figure is seated but alert, with a sword
in his hand and with a child, safe under his protection, asleep against his
knee.

The sculptor, G.H. Paulin of Edinburgh,
was introduced to the town council by A.E.
Hornel, the famous 'Glasgow School' artist
who had strong Kirkcudbright connections.
The statue was cast in the Edinburgh
foundry of McDonald and Creswick, whose
work included the casting of the Hawick
war memorial.

The memorial was unveiled on 14 April
1921, by Colonel R.F. Dudgeon, the Lord
Lieutenant of the county, and dedicated by
the Reverend W. Barclay. Reports of the
ceremony mention that amongst those
present was a veteran of the Crimean War,
the eighty-seven year old Robert Kissock
Cameron.

Photograph courtesy of R. Boorman.

MAXWELLTOWN

O ne of the most moving of all war memorials is that at Maxwelltown, near Dumfries, to the dead of the First World War only.

On a pedestal of granite stands a bronze military figure, the 1921 work of sculptor Henry Price. The young Scottish soldier is in full uniform but without his rifle, and his arms are raised high, above shoulder height, towards heaven, with the palms upwards, as if he were begging for an end to the slaughter of the war.

On the granite, below the figure, are inscribed the names of over 200 men of the burgh who fell in the war, and the words,

PRO PATRIA
IN MEMORY OF THE MEN OF THE BURGH OF
MAXWELLTOWN
AND THE PARISH OF TROQUEER WHO FELL
IN THE GREAT WAR 1914–1919.

That 200 men from such a small burgh could die in the war gives added poignancy to the represented soldier's appeal.

The monument, with a total height of fifteen foot, is in a prominent position at a road junction, and behind it is an attractive and well tended garden of lawns and rose beds, with small trees and park benches.

PRO PATRIA

IN

MEMORY OF THE MEN
OF THE
BURGH OF MAXWELLTOWN
AND THE
PARISH OF TROQUEER
WHO FELL IN THE GREAT WAR

1914 - 1919

CROYDON

The Croydon memorial, on a prominent site by the Town Hall, was designed by James Burford with statues sculpted by P.R. Montford in 1921.

The memorial incorporates both a cenotaph supported by a stone shaft, and two bronze figures seated at the foot. On one side of the monument is a soldier of the East Surrey Regiment, tending his own wounded arm, and on the other is a woman with eyes closed, holding a young child, while seeming to reach out to the injured man.

On the stonework separating them is the inscription,

> A TRIBUTE TO THE MEN AND WOMEN OF CROYDON
> WHO DIED AND SUFFERED.

High above is a bronze cross, immediately under the tomb, and the dates of the two world wars.

A further inscription has recently been added,

> AND IN MEMORY OF THOSE WHO LOST THEIR LIVES
> IN WARS AND CONFLICTS SINCE.

EDGAR MOBBS

Edgar Mobbs, in the years before the Great War, was a local rugby hero who captained the Saints, Northampton's rugby team, played for the Barbarians and was capped for England on seven occasions.

At the outbreak of war he raised a 'Sportsman's Battalion', officially the 7th Battalion Northamptonshire Regiment, and as its Lieutenant Colonel eventually died in 1917 in an attack at Passchendaele.

A memorial to him, by sculptor Alfred Turner, was originally unveiled by Lord Lilford in July 1921 in Northampton's Market Place, and later moved in 1937 to the Garden of Remembrance in Abington Square.

The monument, with a stone base and column, has a bronze bust of Mobbs and panels of scenes from the battlefield and the rugby pitch, surmounted by a bronze figure of the Goddess of Fame.

The memorial is, however, only part of the way in which Edgar Mobbs is commemorated. In 1921 the first Mobbs Memorial match between the East Midlands and the Barbarians was played and eighty years later the match is still an annual event. Each year before the match there is a short ceremony and a wreath in Saints or Barbarian colours is laid at the Mobbs Memorial.

THIS MEMORIAL WAS ERECTED IN

 Macclesfield

The war memorial at Park Green, Macclesfield consists of a beautifully planted and maintained memorial garden within which is an imaginative arrangement of a central stone support for three fine bronze figures, and stone pillars on which are carved the names of the dead.

The main feature is the body of a soldier killed in a gas attack, with his gas mask lying unfitted at his side. Over him leans the figure of Britannia, in the act of placing a laurel wreath. Above them, on the central stone shaft, is the figure of a woman in mourning. The sculptor was J. Millard. In front of the central column are four stone pillars, two to either side, and names of those from the area who fell in the First World War are inscribed on all four sides of each pillar, sixteen sides in all, each with some forty names.

The names of the dead of the Second World War have been added on twelve bronze plaques on walls to the sides of the main base.

Under the figure of the soldier are the words,

THIS MEMORIAL WAS ERECTED IN HONOUR OF MACCLESFIELD MEN WHO GAVE THEIR LIVES FOR THEIR KING AND EMPIRE IN THE GREAT WAR 1914–1918.

The memorial was unveiled on 21 September 1921 by the Mayor, Alderman J.G. Frost, and dedicated by the Bishop of Chester.

$\mathscr{P}$ORTSMOUTH

The appeal by the Mayor of Portsmouth, John Timpson, in a letter to *The Hampshire Telegraph & Post* on 27 December 1918, was both for suggestions as to the type of war memorial which the city should have, and for donations towards a memorial fund.

Eventually almost £30,000 was received, £10,000 of which was allocated as a gift to the Royal Portsmouth Hospital, the balance being set aside for a suitable monument. The design for this was thrown open to competition and from no fewer than fifty designs sent in, an assessor appointed by the British Association of Architects chose that of Messrs Gibson & Gordon of Old Bond Street, London, with sculpture by Charles Sergeant Jagger, a holder of the Military Cross, the artist whose war memorial commissions eventually included those at Bedford, Paddington station, and Hoylake and, his masterpiece, the Royal Artillery memorial in London.

Their design consisted of a central raised cenotaph behind which was a semi-circular twenty-two foot high wall carrying ten name panels, five for the army and five for the navy, and in front of which were two pedestals with pieces of statuary, machine gunners representing respectively the army and the navy. The memorial was basically of Portland stone and the site on which it was erected adjoined the Guildhall.

A bronze plaque in the centre of the wall reads,

THIS MEMORIAL WAS ERECTED BY THE PEOPLE OF
PORTSMOUTH IN PROUD AND LOVING MEMORY OF THOSE
WHO IN THE GLORIOUS MORNING OF THEIR DAYS FOR
ENGLAND'S SAKE LOST ALL BUT ENGLAND'S PRAISE.
MAY LIGHT PERPETUAL SHINE UPON THEM.

Later inscriptions refer to those who lost their lives in the Second World War.

A crowd estimated to be almost 30,000 strong attended the unveiling ceremony by the Duke of Connaught on 19 October 1921.

Of the £10,000 given to the Royal Portsmouth Hospital from the City's war memorial fund, the bulk went into improvements and additions within the hospital, but part was used to improve the entrance to the hospital and to build a new War Memorial Gateway on Commercial Road.

The gateway, opened officially by Princess Helena Victoria on 19 May 1922, unfortunately no longer exists having been demolished comparatively recently, along with the hospital itself, in a major redevelopment of the area.

When the type of memorial that Portsmouth should have was being discussed, the view was put forward forcibly that money spent on the Cenotaph, or other monument, was wasted and that money spent on the hospital was better used, but in the long run, the memorial at Portsmouth still remains as a tribute to the dead, while the improved hospital has ceased to exist.

LONDON & NORTH-WESTERN RAILWAY

At the entrance to Euston railway station, London, is the memorial by R. Wynn Owen to the 3,719 men of the London and North-Western Railway Company who died in the Great War. It also now commemorates the dead of the Second World War who were employees of the London Midland and Scottish Railway, the L.M.S.

Unveiled on 21 October 1921 by Field Marshal Earl Haig, the memorial consists of a stone column on a granite base, with a cross and bronze wreath decorating each of the four sides. There are four bronze servicemen, representing different branches of the armed forces, at the corners of the base. The figures are in mourning with heads lowered and rifles reversed.

At the time of its unveiling the memorial had more space around it but, despite the large modern office block which now dominates the immediate background, the monument is still prominent, and in good condition.

WICKENHAM

The Twickenham memorial, in Radnor Gardens, by the banks of the Thames, was unveiled on Wednesday, 2 November 1921, by Field Marshal Sir William Robertson. There was a large attendance in spite of the drenching rain, and newspaper photographs show a sea of umbrellas at the scene of the unveiling.

In attendance was the Band of the Royal Military School of Music, from nearby Kneller Hall.

The monument takes the form of a bronze figure by Mortimer Brown, on a stone plinth with three bronze relief panels. The figure is of a soldier striding forward with one arm raised high, and waving his cap in greeting. The gesture, and the happy expression on the face, make a strong contrast to the more conventional attitude of mourning, with head bowed and rifle reversed, to be found in many war memorial figures, and the exuberance is reminiscent of 'The Home-Coming' statue in Cambridge.

On the front of the plinth are the inscriptions,

1914–1918. TO THE GLORIOUS MEMORY OF THE
MEN OF TWICKENHAM WHO FELL IN THE GREAT WAR
AND TO THOSE WHO GAVE THEIR LIVES IN
THE WAR OF 1939–1945.

On the other three sides are the bronze panels, with scenes representing the Navy, Air Force and Women's Services.

TALYBRIDGE

The memorial unveiled on 6 November 1921 at Stalybridge, in Cheshire, was designed, appropriately enough, by a native of the town, an eminent London sculptor, Ferdinand Blundstone.

His design, at one end of Victoria Bridge over the River Tame, consists of a pedestal of stone at each side of the bridge, supporting groups of bronze statuary, the total height of each pedestal and bronze being eighteen foot. From each pedestal a five foot high wing wall curves away to end in a smaller pedestal surmounted by a lion. The walls carry the names of the 628 men who gave their lives in the First World War, their names being arranged in regiments.

On the left-hand main pedestal a bronze winged female figure holds an eternal flame over a dying sailor, while the inscription on the stone below reads,

> 1914–1918 JUTLAND. ZEEBRUGGE. THE FALKLAND ISLANDS.
> REMEMBER THE LOVE OF THEM WHO CAME NOT
> HOME FROM THE WAR. SEE TO IT THAT THEY
> SHALL NOT HAVE DIED IN VAIN.

The right-hand pedestal has a bronze group of a similar female figure supporting a fallen soldier, his right hand resting on hers. The inscription below is,

> 1914–1918 THE MARNE. YPRES. THE SOMME. ALL YOU
> WHO PASS BY REMEMBER WITH GRATITUDE THE MEN
> OF STALYBRIDGE WHO DIED FOR YOU.

The Stalybridge public subscription after 1918 raised £6,000 in a few weeks and since this was almost fifty per cent more than the cost of the memorial the surplus was devoted to furthering the education and interests generally of the children of the men who died.

To the original memorial was added, after the Second World War, a further wall similar to the others, with the names, again in regiments, of the dead and with a lion surmounting a stone pedestal on which is carved,

> 1939–1945
> NOW HEAVEN IS BY THE YOUNG INVADED
> THEIR LAUGHTER'S IN THE HOUSE OF GOD.

$\mathscr{P}$ORT SUNLIGHT

From Port Sunlight and the Lever Brothers companies throughout the world, over 4,000 men fought in the war, and of that number 481 were killed.

Their memorial in the centre of Port Sunlight, now surrounded by alternate displays of red and white roses and in an area of lawns and flower beds, is a cross round the base of which are inscribed the names of the fallen with the dedication,

THESE ARE NOT DEAD, SUCH SPIRITS NEVER DIE.

Encircling the foot of the cross a group of bronze sculptured figures symbolises the defence of the home. One soldier stands with fixed bayonet, another kneels to fire and a third, wounded, is about to receive aid from a nurse, while children look on in alarm. The platform supporting the cross is surrounded by a low parapet and at intervals are further bronze groups representing the sea, land and air forces and the Red Cross. Finally, there are figures of children offering garlands in gratitude for the sacrifice made.

The designer of this beautiful and impressive memorial, was the sculptor Sir W. Goscombe John RA who was well served by granite masons Messrs. William Kirkpatrick Limited of Manchester and by the bronze founder Mr A.B. Burton of Thames Ditton. Even by the exceptional standard normally set by the sculptor, the whole work is absolutely outstanding.

The unveiling on 3 December 1921, was by ex-sergeant T.G. Eames who was a former employee of the Company and who had been blinded at the Somme. He was guided and assisted by ex-private R.E. Cruikshank who was awarded the VC in 1918 for his actions in Palestine.

As well as the names on the memorial, the names of all who served and their war records are commemorated both by a book deposited in a cavity in the memorial and by others placed in the Lady Lever Art Gallery and in Christ Church, Port Sunlight, by the Hon. W. Hulme Lever.

The dates of the 1939–1945 war have been added to the original memorial, together with the names of 118 Second World War dead.

OYSTON

The Royston memorial was unveiled in Melbourn Street on Sunday, 26 March 1922 by Lieutenant Colonel E.C.M. Phillips of the Herts & Beds Regiment, who had been a prisoner of war. The sum of £1,580 had been raised by the memorial committee and the resulting monument was unveiled in the presence of an estimated crowd of 3,000 people.

The work was, and still is, a most unusual and beautiful tribute. It is some forty foot long, and its flanking walls are of red brick with flint panels and with Portland stone courses above and below.

The central feature has a bronze soldier of 1914-18 standing in front of a marble group of his military predecessors who are within an archway inscribed with the dates of the Great War. The figures behind are an Agincourt bowman, a medieval knight, an Elizabethan soldier, Thomas Cartwright who was an Elizabethan scholar and worthy of Royston, a Cromwellian Ironside, a soldier of George II and one from Wellington's army at Waterloo. At the feet of the modern soldier is a 'Royston Crow', a symbol of the town since at least the mid-seventeenth century.

The names of the dead of the First World War are on large tablets to the sides of the statuary, while after the Second World War the 1939–1945 dates and the names of the fallen have been added to the plinth on which the bronze figure stands. There would not have been room originally on the plinth for the names of the 1914–18 dead since there were 116 of them compared with 25 in the Second World War. The first name of the first list was a VC, Captain Harold Ackroyd.

The architect and sculptor for this outstanding memorial were respectively Mr. P. Morley Horder and Mr Clemons, both of London, while the local firm of W. Whitehead carried out the monumental masonry work.

$\mathscr{S}$KIPTON

The Skipton memorial is on a prominent roundabout site on the edge of the town centre, and close to Skipton Castle. A bronze winged figure of Victory stands on top of a very tall stone shaft, while at the foot is a very unusual and imaginative bronze warrior, representing Humanity, resting one knee on the ground while he breaks his sword across the other.

Surrounding the work are attractive green and gold painted railings ornamented by laurel wreaths, swords, lion heads and Yorkshire roses.

The monument, originally commemorating some 370 men of the town who died, was designed by John Cassidy of Manchester, who was also responsible for the memorial at Clayton-le-Moors amongst others, and the unveiling ceremony was on 8 April 1922.

An inscription on the stone,

THESE WERE THE BRAVE UNKNOWING HOW TO
YIELD WHO TERRIBLE IN VALOUR KEPT THE FIELD
AGAINST THE FOE AND HIGHER THAN LIFE'S
BREATH PRIZING THEIR HONOUR MET THE DOOM
OF DEATH AND NOW THEY REST PEACEFUL
ENFOLDED IN THEIR COUNTRY'S BREAST.

now carries the dates of both World Wars, and on the memorial are three bronze plaques, two listing the 370 dead of the First World War, and the other the 76 dead of the Second World War.

ACCRINGTON

The Accrington memorial stands high up in a parkland setting, with extensive views before it, views protected by the fact that the land was purchased by the War Memorial Committee to ensure that it would remain without obstruction.

The memorial in Oak Hill Park, off Manchester Road, takes the form of an obelisk of Longridge stone before which stands a beautiful stone female figure representing, according to the Unveiling Ceremony Order of Proceedings, Compassion and Piety. To the sides of the obelisk are columns supporting eternal flames and on the heavy, elaborate base is the inscription,

TO THE HONOURED MEMORY OF THE MEN OF
ACCRINGTON WHO GAVE THEIR LIVES IN THE GREAT WAR.

At a lower level is a wall on which are a dozen Westmorland green slate tablets listing a total of 865 names of the fallen.

The architect for the memorial, built at a cost of £6,885, was Professor C.H. Reilly and the sculptor Tyson Smith of Liverpool, who also worked on the memorials in his home city and in Southport. The unveiling was on 1 July 1922, the anniversary of the first day of the Battle of the Somme, and was performed by Mr. H.H. Bolton JP, a local industrialist who lost three sons in the war. A crowd estimated at 15,000 attended the ceremony and the first wreath was laid by Captain Harwood who, when mayor, raised the Accrington 'Pals' Battalion which suffered such heavy casualties on the Somme.

In 1951 an addition to the original monument was unveiled. A further wall, again bearing green slate panels, this time four in number, lists over 170 dead of 1939–45. An inscription reads,

LET US REMEMBER THOSE WHO IN THEIR LIVES
FOUGHT AND DIED FOR US.

Three further names have subsequently been added, one under 'Northern Ireland', and two under 'Falklands Campaign 1982'.

BRADFORD

The Bradford memorial was unveiled on Saturday, 1 July 1922, the sixth anniversary of the first day of the Battle of the Somme, when the Bradford 'Pals' Battalion of the West Yorkshire Regiment had suffered such heavy casualties.

The unveiling, before a crowd of 40,000, was carried out by Lieutenant-Colonel Alderman Anthony Gadie, a former Lord Mayor who had served in France with the Royal Artillery. The dedication was by the Vicar of Bradford, Archdeacon W. Stanton Jones. Field Marshal Earl Haig, a freeman of the city, was unable to attend, but another freeman, who had been elected on 13 September 1921, to represent all ex-servicemen, ex-sergeant J.W. Robertshaw, took part in the ceremony.

The memorial was in the form of a Cenotaph of Bolton Wood stone, supported by the bronze figures of a solder and a sailor, while high up on the front was a stone cross symbolising Sacrifice.

The designer was the City Architect, Walter Williamson, and the site chosen was the prominent one of Victoria Square, in front of the statue of Queen Victoria.

In addition to the Cenotaph there was a Roll of Honour, with the names of nearly 37,000 Bradford men who served in the war, of whom about 5,000 were killed, and this was placed in the Central Free Library.

The memorial's two bronze figures, moving forward with fixed bayonets, provoked immediate criticism for being too warlike and aggressive. In one evening church service a 'sense of bitter and deep disappointment' was expressed that such figures should be part of the design. The Lord Mayor himself contended that the two figures with fixed bayonets were 'quite out of place' and did not 'strike the right note'. His opinion was that they were 'altogether too ferocious, too aggressive' and did not 'typify the spirit in which so many Bradford men took up arms and even laid down their lives, that the late conflict should be a war to end war'.

In 1969, the offending bayonets were deliberately twisted and bent by either peace campaigners or vandals, and when the memorial was subsequently cleaned, they were not replaced. The figures are still without bayonets which, unfortunately, makes them appear unbalanced and detracts from a fine monument.

After the Second World War the original inscriptions were amended to include the 1939–1945 dates, and the present wording includes 'other conflicts'.

The Cambridgeshire war memorial, on a prominent site in Hills Road, Cambridge, was unveiled on 3 July 1922, by the Duke of York.

An eight foot bronze figure in Cambridgeshire Regiment uniform, it is named 'The Home-Coming' and the stride of the soldier is two inches longer than normal to give the feeling of triumph and elation. On his back is a pack and a captured German helmet, on his left shoulder is his rifle over which is hung a laurel wreath, and in his right hand he is carrying his own helmet and a rose.

The bronze is on a stone base, designed by George Hubbard, and on it are carved coats of arms and the words,

TO THE MEN OF CAMBRIDGESHIRE, THE ISLE OF ELY,
THE BOROUGH AND UNIVERSITY OF CAMBRIDGE,
WHO SERVED IN THE GREAT WAR 1914–1919 AND
IN THE WORLD WAR 1939–1945.

The sculptor of the figure was R. Tait McKenzie who also sculpted the Scottish American memorial in Princes Street, Edinburgh. The figure was modelled in his studio at the University of Pennsylvania and a similar figure was commissioned for Woodbury, New Jersey. The main difference in the two is in the modelling of the heads of the young men. Apparently studies of students at Christ's College were used for the Cambridgeshire memorial while 'an American type' was used for Woodbury.

It seems that the preparations for the unveiling did not proceed without difficulty. The bronze figure was not cast in time and a bronzed plaster replica was used for the ceremony with fears for its reaction to heavy rain. Apparently all went well and the actual bronze was erected ten days later.

$\mathcal{R}$UGBY SCHOOL

At Rugby School the stone of the attractive War Memorial Chapel, which looks out across the famous Close, is in contrast to the brick of the earlier school buildings. The architect was Sir Charles Nicholson, an old boy of the school, and the work was carried out by Wooldridge and Simpson of Oxford.

Inside the chapel, the dedication ceremony for which was on 8 July 1922, is a beautiful cabinet decorated with carving and marquetry and supported by carved columns. It is octagonal in shape and eight shallow glass-fronted drawers contain the volumes of the War Register.

Surmounting this impressive piece is the fine bronze of a young officer with hands clasped before him, head bowed, and on the walls beside the cabinet are carved the names of those who died in the First World War.

A similar cabinet, with a bronze winged figure sheathing his sword, stands before the carved names of those commemorated from the Second World War.

In the area between the main Chapel and the War Memorial Chapel there are stained-glass windows with scenes of the Great War, one of them depicting an officer on horseback urging on his troops. There are also plaques referring to conflicts and losses since 1945.

In the main Chapel itself there is a stained-glass window unveiled on 25 June 1904 to commemorate the dead of the 1899–1902 South African War. This lists twenty-five Old Rugbeians who died, twenty-one of whom were officers and four were other ranks.

ALLERTON

Over 100 men from Allerton, near Bradford, gave their lives in the Great War, and the memorial to them is situated just inside the entrance to Ladyhill Park. £2,000 was raised by public subscription for the monument which was designed by Harold Brownsword of London. A stone pedestal is surmounted by a group of three bronze figures, a boy symbolising 'posterity' offering a laurel wreath in tribute to a soldier supported in the arms of a cowled figure described in contemporary accounts as representing 'Death'.

A lead-lined casket containing newspapers and a selection of contemporary documents was placed under the foundations of the memorial, which was unveiled on 29 July 1922, by Sir James Hill, a freeman of Bradford who had risen from humble beginnings to become Lord Mayor. He had become MP for Bradford Central in 1916, and had been created a Baron in 1917. The dedication was offered by Reverend W.E. Spencer, and a poem specially written for the occasion was read by the poet, Walter Robinson.

The Allerton memorial has in the past suffered from vandalism but, apart from a small amount of graffiti, it is at present in a well maintained condition.

The bronze group is a particularly interesting and imaginative work and its sculptor, Harold Brownsword, who was later principal of Regent Street Polytechnic in London, also designed two other local memorials, at Thornton and Eccleshill.

LEEDS

The City of Leeds had a fine record during the First World War. Its Roll of Honour has over 10,000 names, and not the least of its sacrifices was on the first day of the Battle of the Somme, the 1 July, 1916, when the 15th Battalion West Yorkshire Regiment (the 'Leeds Pals') made an attack on the heavily fortified German Position at Serre but was received with such devastating fire that all its officers were either killed or wounded. Out of a total of 900 men taking part in the attack only seventeen answered the subsequent roll call.

It is all the more surprising, therefore, that appeals for subscriptions for a city war memorial met with such a poor response in the years following the war.

Early suggestions were for expensive projects like an art gallery, a museum, or a children's hospital, and early in 1920, 60,000 circulars were sent out asking for subscriptions with a view to developing an area opposite the Town Hall, in a grandiose scheme likely to cost £500,000 or so. Response was very poor, and so an amended scheme designed by Sir Reginald Blomfield, at an estimated cost of £55,000, was approved.

This also had to be shelved through lack of funds and in February 1921 a desperate appeal by the Mayor for a greatly reduced sum of £20,000 for a Cenotaph and a disabled Soldiers' fund, brought in only £5,300, later to increase to £6,000.

This £6,000 was from only 210 subscribers out of a population of half a million, and three of these subscribers gave £1,000 each. One of these three, Mr. Joseph Clark, suggested that a dozen people should pay for a memorial and that the city should not pretend that the whole of the population had contributed.

Finally, a memorial costing some £5,000 was designed by a London sculptor, Mr. C.H. Fehr, who had been responsible for the city's statue of James Watt in City Square, and whose other war memorial work included Keighley, Colchester and Eastbourne. The new memorial, also sited in City Square, was of white Carrera marble and surmounted by a bronze winged figure of 'Victory' with a sword in her right hand and a wreath in her left. This figure was eleven foot in overall height, from the bronze base to the wing tips. The total height of the monument was thirty-one foot.

On two sides of the plinth were bronze figures representing 'Peace', a female figure holding a dove aloft, and 'War', St George slaying the dragon.

On Saturday, 14 October 1922, the completed memorial was unveiled by Viscount Lascelles and dedicated by the Vicar of Leeds, the Reverend

B.O.F. Heywood. The question of whether the scale of the memorial was appropriate for a city the size of Leeds was set aside and forgotten, and on the day of the ceremony a large crowd filled the square and the surrounding streets, and the monument with its white marble and fine bronzes looked an imposing and fitting tribute.

This, however, was only a temporary state of affairs. To satisfy traffic requirements the monument was moved from City Square and is now sited in a much less prominent position in the Headrow.

The figure of Victory was felt to be unsafe and was removed, therefore reducing the overall height of the memorial by a third. The remainder of the memorial was capped, to disguise the absence of the statue, which was re-erected at Cottingley Crematorium where it was gradually vandalised to the point that it was completely destroyed.

In recent years the capping of the memorial was removed and a new bronze winged female figure has now taken the place of the original.

The bronze female figure, representing 'Peace'.

St George slaying the dragon, representing 'War'.

The original Victory figure, now completely destroyed.

The memorial with its temporary stone capping.

$\mathscr{S}$TREATHAM

Streatham's war memorial was dedicated and unveiled in the Garden of Remembrance at the corner of Streatham Common, on Saturday, 14 October 1922. A crowd of some 5,000 attended as General Sir Charles Monro unveiled the monument which was dedicated by the Bishop of Southwark.

The garden is a pleasant one laid out on two levels with attractive trees, grass and flower beds, and with wooden benches. It is on a very busy corner with heavy traffic but perhaps the loss of a quiet atmosphere is offset by the prominence of the memorial.

The garden is dominated by the bronze life-sized statue of a bare-headed soldier with head bowed and rifle reversed, on a stone plinth and with a low stone and metal railing surround.

The bronze was sculpted by Albert Toft whose other memorial work included that in Leamington, Birmingham, Holborn, Oldham, Thornton Cleveleys and France.

In addition to the garden and the statue, public subscription provided for a Roll of Honour, with the names of 720 or so who died, to be placed in the Streatham Library, and for a house adjoining the Garden of Remembrance, 'The Chimes', to be used as a United Services Club. The House was eventually destroyed during the air raids of the Second World War.

The dates of the Second World War have since been added to the base of the memorial in similar style to the original.

ℰNNISKILLEN

The Fermanagh War Memorial in Enniskillen was unveiled on 25 October 1922, at a turbulent time in Ireland's history.

The Irish Free State came into being that year but civil war followed, and by August Michael Collins had been assassinated by Anti-Treaty Republicans.

The memorial was unveiled by the last Lord Lieutenant of all-Ireland, Viscount Fitzalan, with a Guard of Honour drawn from the Lincolnshire Regiment, the Inniskilling Fusiliers, and the Royal Horse Artillery. Four Inniskilling senior NCOs stood at the corners of the monument with arms reversed.

The memorial, a bronze soldier figure supported by a high stone plinth, commemorated some 600 men of Fermanagh, half of them Royal Inniskilling Fusiliers.

Tragically it was the scene on Remembrance Sunday, 8 November 1987, of an IRA bombing which resulted in the death of eleven people of the town. The explosion, at 10.45 that morning, destroyed St. Michael's Reading Room, the local community centre, and brought part of it crashing down on the crowd waiting for the Remembrance Ceremony which was soon to have taken place a few yards away.

Debris covered the area and flying fragments pockmarked the stonework of the memorial, inscribed with the names of the war dead. Bandsmen left their pipes and drums to search with bare hands for bodies and survivors amongst the ruins.

Two weeks later, on Sunday, 22 November, with the debris cleared away and the site of the explosion boarded up, the Remembrance Ceremony finally took place, in front of a huge crowd. The ceremony was attended by the Prime Minister and a photograph taken that day shows Mrs. Thatcher laying a wreath at the base of the memorial beneath its bronze figure, with head bowed and rifle reversed, of an Inniskilling Fusilier, whose regimental motto was NEC ASPERA TERRENT (neither do difficulties deter).

In recent years the memorial has been re-designed to add extra height and to the names of the dead, inscribed afresh, have been added the names of the dead of 1939–45, all on bronze plates. In addition, designers Richard Pierce and Philip Flanagan have added a dignified tribute to the eleven dead of 1987. Eleven bronze doves now circle in flight closely around the top of the plinth, each individually shaped but all flying upwards.

Mrs. Thatcher laying a wreath at Enniskillen.

Photograph by kind permission of *The Times*, London. Copyright, 22 November 1987

HOYLAKE & WEST KIRBY

It is difficult to imagine a more striking setting for a war memorial than the site on Grange Hill, West Kirby, where the Hoylake and West Kirby Memorial was unveiled in December 1922. High up on the Wirral peninsular it looks out over the sea on three sides, with views to Liverpool and North Wales.

A forty foot high obelisk of Cornish granite has at its base two bronze figures. One represents Humanity, a female figure holding a wreath of thorns and with broken chains hanging from her wrists, symbolising the bondage with which she was threatened. The other is a soldier figure typical of the work of the sculptor, Charles Sergeant Jagger. With feet astride and with his rifle and bayonet held in both hands across his body, he conveys determination, toughness and a will to win. On the ground in front of him lies a German helmet.

To avoid vandalism the bayonet attached to the soldier's rifle is now affixed only for the Remembrance Day ceremony, and then immediately removed.

Round the shaft of the memorial above the heads of the bronzes, are engraved the words of Kipling,

WHO STANDS IF FREEDOM FALL?
WHO DIES IF ENGLAND LIVES?

On the plinth are the inscriptions,

IN GRATITUDE TO GOD AND
TO THE MEN AND WOMEN FROM
THESE PARTS WHO LAID DOWN
THEIR LIVES IN THE GREAT WAR
1914–1919 – 1939–1945
THEY WERE A WALL UNTO US
BOTH BY NIGHT AND DAY.

and

AT THE CALL OF KING AND COUNTRY THEY LEFT
ALL THAT WAS DEAR TO THEM, ENDURED HARDNESS,
FACED DANGER, AND FINALLY PASSED OUT OF THE SIGHT
OF MEN BY THE PATH OF DUTY AND SELF SACRIFICE,
GIVING THEIR OWN LIVES THAT OTHERS MIGHT LIVE
IN FREEDOM. LET THOSE WHO COME AFTER SEE TO
IT THAT THEIR NAMES ARE NOT FORGOTTEN.

#
OLDHAM

The First World War Memorial in Oldham was erected on Church Terrace outside St. Mary's Church. The 26 foot high monument was designed by sculptor Albert Toft and its central feature was a 14 foot high group of bronze soldiers. This exceptional work was said to be one of the largest pieces of bronze sculpture to be cast and founded at the time.

The group was mounted on a heavy base of grey granite within which was a chamber with access through two bronze doors.

On 28 April 1923, the memorial was unveiled by General Sir Ian Hamilton, former Chief-of-Staff to Lord Kitchener, and dedicated by the Bishop of Manchester, in the presence of a crowd of some 10,000. The General, as was his wont, made a slightly controversial speech, in which he anticipated the difficulties that would result from the severity of the terms of the Treaty of Versailles.

After the Second World War the base of the memorial was altered by the removal of one of the doors and the construction of a glass-fronted chamber holding a Book of Remembrance for the fallen of 1939–1945, the pages being turned mechanically. Both the book and the turning mechanism were donated in 1955 by Ferranti, a major employer in the town at that time. The treatment of names is quite different to that of the Great War names which are recorded on bronze plaques on the wall of the churchyard behind the monument, and is a more thoughtful addition to an earlier memorial than the usual mere changes in inscription.

In the stonework above the glass front are the words,

DEATH IS THE GATE OF LIFE
1914–1918   1939–1945.

 CROMPTON

T he bronze group which dominates the war memorial of Crompton, near Oldham, is by the sculptor Richard R. Goulden, a former captain in the Royal Engineers. His other works include the figure of St. Christopher which is the war memorial of the Bank of England, the war memorial figures at Dover, Redhill and Reigate, and Kingston-upon-Thames, and the eponymous winged and armoured saint with sword raised at the Parish Church of St. Michael's, Cornhill, in the City of London.

The Crompton memorial is similar in theme to that at Cornhill, and the bronze group represents man protecting the future generation in the form of little children, and clearing from their path perils in the symbolic form of wild, savage animals.

The statue is on a plinth of Scottish granite on the front of which is the inscription in bronze letters,

IN MEMORY OF THE MEN OF CROMPTON WHO FOUGHT
AND GAVE THEIR LIVES TO FREE MANKIND FROM THE
OPPRESSION AND BRUTAL TYRANNY OF WAR.
1914–1918   1939–1945

On the sides of the base are Rolls of Honour in sculptured bronze, each 5 foot in height and with relief panels depicting the heads of men from the various services. On these rolls are the names of 346 men who fell in the First World War including Alfred, Charles and Richard Hopley. Mrs Hopley, who had eight sons serving in the war, laid one of the official wreaths when the memorial was unveiled by General Sir Ian Hamilton and dedicated by the Vicar of Shaw, the Reverend A.R. Mackintosh.

On the rear of the monument a bronze plaque has been added with the names of the dead of the Second World War.

Built into the structure, between the bronze and the granite, was a

sealed lead casket containing a variety of items including six coins from a sovereign to a penny, three cops of cotton locally spun, a length of fustian cloth manufactured locally, wartime ration cards and coupons issued by the Ministry of Food, a programme of the local peace celebrations on 19 July 1919, a Coronation medal and a peace medal, the first report of the Crompton Disabled Sailors and Soldiers Association, the 1922–23 yearbook of the Crompton Urban District Council, the *Crompton Tradesman's Almanac*, a retail price list of provisions, a copy of the local newspaper, the names of the three oldest inhabitants of the area and a summary of the war memorial scheme from its inception.

As well as funding the cost of the memorial and its pleasant surrounding small park, the memorial committee also raised enough money after 1918 to make grants to the children and dependants of the fallen.

TONEHAVEN

The war memorial at Stonehaven, near Aberdeen, stands high on the Black Hill overlooking the town, the sea and the nearby ruins of Dunnottar Castle.

Designed by John Ellis, a Stonehaven architect, the memorial is a most unusual temple-like structure, open to the sky, with six massive pillars and resting on a base of rough boulders. It commands wonderful views and conveys a marked atmosphere of isolation and tranquillity.

The land for the memorial was gifted by Lord and Lady Cowdray, and Lady Cowdray herself performed the unveiling ceremony on Sunday, 20 May 1923, when more than 3,000 people attended.

Inside the walls a granite memorial stone weighing over ten tons carries the names of the 162 who died in the war, sixty-two of them being Gordon Highlanders and one being a woman, a nursing sister.

Above the doorway is the inscription,

ERECTED BY THE PEOPLE OF STONEHAVEN AND DISTRICT
A TRIBUTE TO THE DEAD. 1914 – 1919.

and inside are the words,

ONE BY ONE DEATH CHALLENGED THEM, ONE BY ONE
THEY SMILED IN HIS GRIM VISAGE AND REFUSED
TO BE DISMAYED.

Carved on the outside are the names of some of the major actions of the war,

MONS, YPRES, VIMY, SOMME, MARNE, ZEEBRUGGE,
GALLIPOLI and JUTLAND.

After the Second World War a similar treatment was given to later battles with names such as DUNKIRK, BATTLE OF BRITAIN, EL ALAMEIN, NORMANDY BEACHES and BURMA being carved on the interior. Also added after 1945 were smaller granite memorial stones in the interior with the names of the dead of 1939–45.

$\mathcal{Y}$ORK & LANCASTER REGIMENT

The memorial in Sheffield to the men of the York and Lancaster Regiment is in Weston Park, between the University and the Mappin Art Gallery.

This striking monument has two main inscriptions on its granite base. The first is,

> TO THE EVERLASTING HONOUR AND GLORY OF THE 8814 OFFICERS NON-COMMISSIONED OFFICERS AND MEN OF THE YORK AND LANCASTER REGIMENT WHO FELL IN THE GREAT WAR 1914–1919.

Below are the words,

> ALSO OF THE 1222 MEMBERS OF THE REGIMENT WHO FELL IN THE WAR 1939–1945.

The numbers commemorated illustrate dramatically the comparative infantry casualty figures in the two wars.

The tall granite column rising from the base is surmounted by a bronze winged figure of Victory, and in support at the sides of the base are the bronze figures of an officer with drawn revolver, and of a private, with sleeves rolled up and with his rifle and helmet slung over his shoulders. Carved into the granite is the regimental badge and at the front and rear are sculptured impedimenta of war; weapons, helmet, greatcoat, drum, ammunition box, flag and so on.

Two local sculptors were commissioned for the work, G.N. Morewood being responsible for the figures of Victory and the officer, while Roy Smith executed the figure of the private.

The unveiling by Field Marshal Lord Plumer, and the dedication by the Bishop of Sheffield, were on Saturday, 7 July 1923.

LOUGHBOROUGH

When the population of Loughborough was asked to vote for their choice of war memorial on 6 November 1919, they had three possibilities before them. The first was some form of conventional monument, the second was a health centre, and the third, most unusually, was a tower and carillon. With great enterprise and despite the high cost, they voted by a majority for the carillon and for the design by William Tapper, the consulting architect to York Minster and architect to Eton College.

Claimed as the only Municipal Grand Carillon in Great Britain, its total cost was finally almost £20,000, an enormous sum for a town of Loughborough's size. A contract to build the bell-tower for £10,500 was placed with the local firm William Moss & Sons Limited, and the order for the carillon was placed with the well known local firm of founders John Taylor & Sons. The cost of the forty-seven bells was £7,000, towards which Messrs. Taylors themselves contributed £2,000. Eventually almost all of the bells were given by either individuals or local organisations.

The main tower is built of small two inch red bricks with a base of Portland stone. The upper part of the construction is of wood covered with copper and consists of a main gallery, a smaller octagonal gallery and a domed roof surmounted by a ball and golden cross. The total height of the tower to the top of the cross is 151 foot. Almost all of the contracts, except for the copper work, were carried out by local firms using local labour.

The memorial was unveiled in Queen's Park on Sunday, 22 July 1923 by Field Marshal Sir William Robertson, and the Bishop of Peterborough pronounced the dedication. On that day the carillon of forty-seven bells was first played by Chevalier Jef Denyn of Malines, Belgium, Sir Edward Elgar having composed 'Memorial Chimes' for the opening recital.

The total weight of the forty-seven bells is 21 tons, the largest being 82 cwts. and the smallest 20 lbs. The dimensions of the largest are sixty inches in height and 72 inches in diameter while the smallest is 7½ inches in height and 7 inches in diameter.

Inscriptions on the individual bells give information about the donors, and in some cases, men commemorated. The largest bell is inscribed,

'In proud, loving memory of his three nephews, killed in action in
France, John William Taylor, Courcelette, 1916;
Gerard Bardsley Taylor, St. Quentin 1918; Arnold Bradley Taylor,
Contalmaison 1916; sons of John William Taylor (1853-1919),
grandsons of John William Taylor (1827-1906), Edmund Denison
Taylor, the founder of these bells, gives this the largest, 1923.'

Other inscriptions include the following,

'The gift of the Engineering and Allied Trades of Loughborough.'

'The gift of the Building and Allied Trades of Loughborough.'

(the cost of trade bells was generally raised by small weekly contributions by men and women in these industries).

'The gift of the sons of William and Anne Moss, Third Mayor and Mayoress of this Borough, two of whose grandsons Howard James Harding Moss (2nd Lieutenant 5th Leicesters) and Gerald Alec Moss (2nd Lieutenant 2nd Manchesters) fell in the Great War.'

'The gift of the Loughborough Grammar School (Past and Present) in memory of the fifty-seven Old Boys who fell in the Great War.'

'Given by Charles and Florence Wightman in memory of Lieutenant John F. Wightman, RAF, killed in action 4 September 1917, aged 18.'

'The gift of Thomas Bowley Garton, MC, in thankfulness for safe return.'

'The gift of Loughborough Corporation Workmen, in memory of F. Bishop, F.C. Fletcher, E. Grant.'

'The gift of Old Comrades of the Church Lads' Brigade.'

Bronze tablets on the base of the tower list the dead of both World Wars and subsequent conflicts. Four tablets carry the names of the 480 who fell in 1914–18, while two suffice for the dead of 1939–45, some 180 in number. There is also one name for each of the wars in Korea, Cyprus and the Falklands.

The inscription for the Second World War reads,

IN HONOURED MEMORY ALSO OF THE MEN
OF LOUGHBOROUGH WHOSE NAMES ARE RECORDED
ON THESE TABLETS AND WHO, FOLLOWING THEIR ELDER
BROTHERS COMMEMORATED BY THIS TOWER, GAVE
THEIR LIVES IN THE SECOND GREAT WAR.

1939 – 1945 PRO PATRIA.

THEIR NAME LIVETH FOR EVERMORE.

The park, in which the tower stands, shows it to its best possible advantage, with avenues, lawns and flower beds all perfectly maintained and with every view of the memorial an impressive one.

EXETER

Amongst the most beautiful of First World War memorials is that of Exeter. The main bronze figure of 'Victory' was in fact given pride of place in the Royal Academy Exhibition of 1922, dominating the quadrangle giving access to Burlington House, and a further bronze of a prisoner of war was also exhibited and highly praised that year. One reviewer stated 'Exeter will be happy in the possession of a war memorial of unparalleled distinction'.

The completed work, in fact, has four bronze figures decorating a massive base and pedestal of Devonshire granite which is surmounted by the 8 foot tall figure of Victory standing upon a dragon, with a sword in her left hand and a laurel in the right, and with her right arm extended above her head. As well as The Prisoner of War, the figures on the base are The Soldier, The Sailor and The Nurse.

The sculptor and designer was Mr. John Angel, a native of Exeter, and the figures were cast by Mr. A.B. Burton of Thames Ditton (Victory and Prisoner of War) and by Mr. William Morris of Brixton (Soldier, Sailor and Nurse). The Exeter architects, Messrs. Greenslade & Challice, co-operated in the design of the pedestal, which was raised and worked by Easton & Son of Exeter. The whole monument is 31 foot high from the base to the laurel, and stands in a commanding position on Northernhay with the ruins of Rougement Castle in the background.

The memorial was unveiled on 24 July 1923, by Admiral of the Fleet Earl Beatty and dedicated by the Bishop of Crediton. Earl Beatty had earlier been made a Freeman of the City, the second admiral to be so honoured, the first having been Nelson after his victory at the Nile in 1801.

IN PROUD AND GRATEFUL MEMORY OF THE MEN WH

A casket containing the names of the 970 who had given their lives in the war, had been placed in a cavity within the memorial, and these names were also inscribed in a book to be kept in the city archives.

Around the plinth are the words,

IN PROUD AND GRATEFUL MEMORY OF THE MEN AND
WOMEN OF EXETER AND OF DEVON WHO GAVE THEIR
LIVES IN THE GREAT WAR 1914–18.
THEIR NAME LIVETH FOR EVERMORE.

while a bronze plate, subsequently added, reads,

THIS TABLET IS DEDICATED TO THE MEMORY OF THOSE
WHO FELL IN THE SECOND WORLD WAR 1939–45.

IN MEMORY OF
MEN AND WOMEN
OF THIS BOROUGH
WHO GAVE THEIR
LIVES IN THE
TWO WORLD WARS

1914   1919   COURAGE

1939   1945

REIGATE AND REDHILL

T he war memorial for Reigate and Redhill took the form of a Memorial Sports Ground at London Road, Redhill, and also a monument erected at Shaw's Corner between the two present town centres.

Admiral of the Fleet Earl Beatty performed the unveiling ceremony on Sunday, 5 August 1923, before proceeding to London Road to declare the Sports Ground 'open to the use of the public for ever, to commemorate the gallant deeds and sacrifices of those connected with the Borough who fell in the Great War'.

The monument features a bronze figure which is typical of the work of Richard R. Goulden, and very similar to his memorial in the Garden of Remembrance in Kingston-upon-Thames. The figure is of a man struggling through briars while carrying a child in one arm and holding aloft a flaming torch with the other. His face is set and gaunt.

An inscription plate explains,

'The bronze represents the triumphant struggle of mankind against the difficulties that beset him in the path of life. Shielding and bearing onward the child, the figure holds aloft the symbol of self-sacrifice to light the way. The flaming cross is used to indicate the suffering endured by men in the war. Flames consume the flesh: the spirit is unconquerable.'

The work is supported by a granite plinth on which, in bronze, are the words COURAGE, HONOUR and SELF-SACRIFICE on three sides and the inscription, again in bronze, on the front,

IN MEMORY OF MEN AND WOMEN OF THIS BOROUGH WHO
GAVE THEIR LIVES IN THE TWO WORLD WARS.
1914–1919   1939–1945

The obelisk that is the Harrogate memorial was erected in 1923 on land formerly known as 'Prospect Gardens', the garden of the Prospect Hotel, which the council had bought for road widening for the sum of £5,000. After the road scheme had been completed a suitable site for a memorial remained.

A subscription list was opened and the required amount for the memorial of some £5,500 was raised.

The design of the chosen architects, J.C. Prestwick and Sons of Leigh, was of a stone obelisk resting on a pedestal, in height seventy-five foot, and with a base sixteen foot square. Bronze tablets on the north and south sides of the pedestal list the names of the 841 men and women from the town who died in the Great War, and on the east and west are carved relief panels by Gilbert Ledward, the artist whose other war memorial work included that at Blackpool, Stockport, Abergavenny, in Westminster Abbey and, most notably, on the Guards' Memorial in London. In the late 1920s he was appointed Professor of Sculpture at the Royal College of Art.

The Harrogate memorial brochure described Ledward's two panels as,

> '1914 – The Call to Arms, a bugler on a battlefield sounding the attack, with a flag in his left hand', and '1918 – Britannia draped in The Flag holding out the laurel wreath of Victory whilst in the foreground bayonets are raised in salute by the men'.

The memorial was unveiled on Saturday, 1 September 1923, by the Earl of Harewood, and dedicated by the Bishop of Ripon, Dr. J.B. Strong. Also present were Lady Harewood, Princess Mary and Viscount Lascelles.

Inscriptions have since been added to include the Second World War and subsequent hostilities.

Today the site is still an open and prominent one, with lawns and flower beds, on the edge of the famous Stray and surrounded by fine buildings.

NORTHUMBERLAND FUSILIERS

One of the finest of all British war memorials, known as 'The Response', stands in the centre of Newcastle close to the Church of St Thomas the Martyr.

Designed by Sir William Goscombe John, with masonry, all in Shap granite, by William Kirkpatrick Ltd., it was a gift to the city from Sir George and Lady Renwick to commemorate the raising of several battalions of the Northumberland Fusiliers. The unveiling, by the Prince of Wales, took place in 1923.

On one side of the memorial are relief stone figures of St George, the patron saint of the regiment, flanked by figures of a Northumberland Fusilier of the Great War and one in the uniform of 1674, the year in which the regiment was enrolled. There are also the arms of Newcastle and Gateshead and the inscription,

TO COMMEMORATE THE RAISING OF THE B COY. 9TH BATT.
AND THE 16TH, 18TH AND 19TH SERVICE BATTALIONS
NORTHUMBER FUSILIERS, BY THE NEWCASTLE AND
GATESHEAD CHAMBER OF COMMERCE AUG.–OCT. 1914.

On the other side of the memorial is a wonderful bronze group twenty-three foot long and about seven foot high, rising to twelve foot high to the top of a trumpeting figure. The group shows Tyneside men in the 'rush to the Colours' which typified the early days of the war. Northumberland Fusiliers, accompanied by two drummer boys, lead the procession and they are followed by other men, in uniform or in working clothes, carrying rifles or tools, some saying goodbye to their families, others waving enthusiastically. Above them, flags fly and a winged 'Renown', symbolising the fame of the regiment, sounds a horn.

The whole scene is both inspiring and moving, and there are many small episodes, such as a boy carrying his father's kit-bag, a workman hugging his wife and baby, and a soldier saying farewell to his younger sister, which must, with hindsight, have seemed unbearably poignant to many of those seeing them for the first time, several years after the war.

On the base of the memorial are the words,

NON SIBI SED PATRIAE. (Not for self but for country) and

THE RESPONSE – 1914.

95

NEWCASTLE

Newcastle's war memorial scheme commenced with the inauguration in 1920 of a 'Shilling Fund' to raise the required finance for a suitable tribute. The target was 300,000 shillings and day after day, for weeks, the papers were full of lists of subscribers and news of progress towards the required figure.

The amount aimed at was achieved in a surprisingly short time and the final figure was well over £16,000.

The monument subsequently commissioned was designed by Mr. C.L. Hartwell, and is identical to his memorial to the men of Marylebone, London. Its main feature is a bronze group of St. George, the Patron Saint of the Northumberland Fusiliers, mounted on a rearing horse, and in the act of killing with his lance the dragon beneath the horse's hooves. The bronze is on a high stone base, the overall height of the memorial being thirty-two foot of which the bronze group is about one third.

On the front of the base is the figure of a lion cut into the stone, and at each side is a bronze panel, one representing 'Peace' and the other 'Justice'.

On the back of the base are the inscriptions,

MEMORY LINGERS HERE.   and
A TRIBUTE OF AFFECTION TO THE MEN OF NEWCASTLE AND DISTRICT WHO GAVE THEIR LIVES IN THE CAUSE OF FREEDOM. THEIR NAME LIVETH FOR EVERMORE.

The memorial cost £13,260 and the balance of over £3,000 was passed to the Governors of the Royal Victoria Infirmary, Newcastle, for the provision and endowment of additional beds, with the stipulation that preferential use of the beds should be reserved for ex-servicemen who were recommended for treatment.

The monument was unveiled in Eldon Square on Wednesday, 26 September 1923, by Field Marshal Earl Haig who, after several other official duties in the city later visited the memorial 'The Response', given to the city by Sir George and Lady Renwick, and expressed his approval of its realism. The last words of Earl Haig's speech before he carried out the unveiling were, 'I unveil this memorial to the memory of brave sons of Newcastle and Northumberland who exchanged the close comradeship of battle for the greater comradeship of immortality'.

The dates of 1939–1945 have now been added to the front of the memorial and in recent years improved landscaping has been carried out, and low railings now protect the stonework.

1914 - 1918
1939 - 1945

FAITHFUL · UNTO · DEATH

ON FAME'S ETERNAL CAMPING GROUND THEIR SILENT TENTS ARE SPREAD
AND GLORY GUARDS WITH SOLEMN ROUND THE BIVOUAC OF THE DEAD

ORNOCH

The war memorial in Dornoch, Sutherland, is one of many fine works by Alexander Carrick. The 8 foot high bronze of a Seaforth Highlander, originally entitled 'After the Battle', has the soldier with one hand raised to shield his eyes from the light as he looks out towards Dornoch Firth.

The statue is supported by a heavy stone pillar with bronze name plates and with the inscription,

ON FAME'S ETERNAL CAMPING GROUND
THEIR SILENT TENTS ARE SPREAD
AND GLORY GUARDS WITH SOLEMN ROUND
THE BIVOUAC OF THE DEAD.

Three bronze plates list sixty-nine First World War dead, of whom forty-one were Seaforth Highlanders. A fourth plate commemorates thirty-one dead of 1939–45.

The unveiling ceremony was on Monday, 29 October 1923 and was performed by Mrs. McDonald, the widow of Captain W.A. McDonald who was mentioned in Dispatches and whose name appears on the memorial.

In recent years the monument has been moved from its position in the centre of a busy junction to a site at the side of the road where it is now floodlit, with a paved surround and rose borders. As is normal under these circumstances, the re-siting was not universally popular.

Sculptor Alexander Carrick RSA, RBS, 1882–1966, was responsible for many war memorials, mostly in Scotland, both in bronze and stone.

Those in bronze include Dornoch and two great-coated soldiers at Walkerburn in the Scottish Borders and at Blairgowrie in Perthshire, both soldiers with arms reversed, coat collars up and heads bowed. Quite different works are the group symbolic of peace on the Frazerburgh monument and the Angel of Peace in Berwick.

Those in stone include Highland figures at St. Margaret's Hope in the Orkneys, at Killin in Perthshire and at Loch Awe where the statue stands at the water's edge. The Oban memorial by him is of two Highlanders carrying a wounded comrade.

It is, however, for his work on the Scottish National War Memorial at Edinburgh Castle that Carrick is perhaps best known. On the front elevation of this building the two figures of 'Justice' and 'Courage' are his, while, inside, the bronze panels to the Royal Engineers and the Royal Artillery (in which he himself served) are also his works.

UNTINGDON

Huntingdon's war memorial, a statue known as 'The Thinking Soldier', was unveiled by the Lord Lieutenant of the County, the Earl of Sandwich, on Armistice Sunday 1923 in the presence of some 3,000 people.

It was appropriate that the new mayor, Colonel M.D. Barclay, who served in the Great War as well as in the South African war, should as his first public duty play a leading part in the day. Another veteran, the Archdeacon of Huntingdon, wearing his war medals as Chaplain of the Forces, read the opening sentences of the ceremony.

The bronze statue of the memorial is of a soldier deep in thought, with his chin supported by his left hand, the left arm in turn supported by a bent left knee. His right hand is on his rifle and his extended right foot is represented as heavily covered in mud. His equipment is particularly finely detailed.

In recent years the area around the memorial has been pedestrianised and an attractive metal post and chain fence now surrounds the base. The inscription in the stone now reads,

TO THE MEN OF 1914-1918 WHO WROUGHT FOR MANKIND
A GREAT DELIVERANCE.

and   ALSO TO THOSE WHO IN 1939-1945 SERVED AND DIED
TO PRESERVE OUR GLORIOUS HERITAGE.

On the reverse is,

TO THOSE WHO IN MANY WARS AND CONFLICTS SINCE
1945 SERVED AND DIED TO PRESERVE FREEDOM.

At its unveiling the memorial was immediately acclaimed as a beautiful and inspiring tribute. A gift from the Huntingdon Federation of Women's Institutes, it was sculpted by Kathleen Scott, the widow of Scott of the Antarctic. The artist must have received undue attention from the press as she apparently addressed the *Huntingdonshire Post* photographer as 'You awful man', a fact that the newspaper was surprisingly happy to report.

In the press report of the ceremony particular mention was made of the wreaths and other floral tributes which were placed at the foot of the memorial, with simple bunches of flowers next to official wreaths such as the Lord Lieutenant's. Unusually, an attempt was made to provide a comprehensive list of these tributes amongst which were,

'In remembrance, from the officers, warrant officers, NCOs and men,
5th Huntingdonshire Regiment.'

'Huntingdon Branch British Legion. In undying memory of our
unconquered comrades who gave their lives for our safety.
Au Revoir. Till Gabriel sounds the Rally.'

'In loving memory of those Wesleyan lads who nobly fought for their
country but did not return.'

'In remembrance, 2nd Hunts. Grammar School Scouts and Cubs.'

'From the Huntingdon Town Football Club to our fallen comrades who
"played the game".'

'In devoted memory of my Billie – Mrs W.P. Markwich.'

'In loving memory of dear Oscar and Oliver from father, mother
and brothers and sisters.'

'To our dear daddy from his little children.
Bertie and Connie Strangward.'

MAIRIDH·AN·CLIU·AGUS
AN·AINM·GU·SIORRUIDH

1914–1918

ARGYLL & SUTHERLAND HIGHLANDERS

BELL·D·PTE	McGREGOR·D·PTE
BLACK·H·PTE	McINTYRE·G·SGT
BRUCE·D·C.S.M	McINTYRE·H·PTE
BUCHANAN·D·A·PTE	MACKAY·A·C·PTE
CAMERON·D·LIEUT	McKINNON·A·PTE
CAMERON·J·M.M·PTE	McLACHLAN·G·P·PTE
CLARKSON·J·J·LIEUT	McLEAN·J·PTE
FORBES·W·S·LIEUT	MACLENNAN·H·L·C.S.M
FORGRIEVE·R·PTE	McNAUGHTON·J·PTE
GRANT·D·M·LIEUT	McNEILL·J·PTE
HICKS·J·PTE	MACNEILL·N·LT.·LT.COL
JAMIESON·D·A·PTE	McPHAIL·A·PTE
JOHNSTONE·A·VC5	McPHAIL·J·A·PTE
KENNEDY·H·W·PTE	MACRAE·M·PTE
LAMB·R·C.Q.M.S	McTAGGART·A·PTE
MAXTON·D·PTE	McVICAR·D·SUB
MORRISON·A·PTE	NEWTON·A·PTE
MACARTHUR·D·A·PTE	NIVEN·W·G·VC5
McCOLL·D·VC5	PKYDE·G·VC5
McCORQUODALE·D·PTE	ROBERTSON·G·PTE
McDONALD·M·VC5	STEVENSON·J·R·SUB
McDONALD·P·PTE	STEWART·W·PTE
McFARLANE·T·VC5	THOMSON·H·PTE
McGILVRAY·A·VC5	WATT·D·PTE
McGILVRAY·J·D·LIEUT	WRIGHT·M·PTE

YEOMAN·J·PTE

1939–1945

YEOMAN·THOMAS·PTE·R.E

$\mathcal{O}$BAN

The Oban Memorial was unveiled on the fifth anniversary of the signing of the Armistice, 11 November 1923, on the Plateau at the end of the Corran Esplanade, before a crowd of several thousands, despite the wet weather.

The unveiling was carried out by Lieutenant Colonel W.H. MacAlpine-Leng, commander of the 13th Highland(Pack)Brigade, and the prayer of dedication was offered by the Right Reverend Kenneth MacKenzie, Bishop of Argyll and the Isles. A piper then played the lament *Lochaber No More* and a trumpeter sounded *The Last Post*.

The memorial, one of sculptor Alexander Carrick's finest works in stone, consists of an unusual and striking group of two Highlanders carrying a wounded comrade between them, the group surmounting a ten foot high cairn of rough granite boulders. To one side of the cairn is a huge prehistoric glacial boulder.

Bronze panels list 173 Great War dead of the Burgh, one of whom was a VC, Highland Light Infantry sergeant, J. Turnbull. The dead are recorded by regiment, 51 of them being Argyll and Sutherland Highlanders.

Further bronze panels below the original ones list the dead of 1939–45, these being in alphabetical order, with the units recorded after each name. One Falkland War name has been added.

Recently the monument has been renovated, with a new paved surround and the lettering now in gold.

THORNTON-CLEVELEYS

The war memorial at Thornton-Cleveleys, near Blackpool, is in a prominent position at Four Lane Ends, Victoria Road, and is surrounded by the lawns and flower beds of a tidy and attractive Garden of Remembrance.

The work of sculptor Albert Toft, the monument consists of a bronze figure of an infantryman on a pedestal of Cornish granite. The soldier stands with bowed head and rifle reversed and with his helmet at his feet. On the plinth are listed the names of the eighty-four Great War dead of the area.

The unveiling ceremony was performed on Sunday, 11 November 1923, Armistice Day, by Lieutenant-General Sir Hugh Jeudwine, the Director-General of the Territorial Army, and former Commander of the 55th Division. In his speech the general referred to the fact that many of the men commemorated had served with him and he was a personal witness to their courage and spirit.

To the original central memorial have been added, in an unusually imaginative treatment, three massive open books, on the pages of which are engraved the names of the 1939–45 dead. The books are between flower beds and opposite the front and sides of the statute, and the distinct impression is of a memorial constructed entirely at one time.

OUNDLE SCHOOL

The Chapel of Oundle School was built in 1922–3 to the perpendicular-style design of the architect A.C. Blomfield, and is dedicated to the memory of those members of the school who gave their lives in the Great War. It was consecrated by the Bishop of Peterborough on 22 November 1923.

A magnificent building surrounded by lawns, the chapel has at the east end an ambulatory in which now there are memorial books and inscribed tablets to the dead of both wars, together with a series of stained-glass windows by Hugh Easton depicting the Seven Ages of Man. Easton was the designer responsible for the Battle of Britain window in Westminster Abbey, and his other work included the Rolls Royce, Biggin Hill and Vyner memorials. His Oundle windows were dedicated by the Bishop of Peterborough on 17 June 1950. The Books of Remembrance, one for each war, have photographs and biographies of each of the men who died, the entries being in alphabetical order.

There are also individual memorials within the ambulatory, including one to three members of the Shepley family 'who within the space of one year gave their lives for their country 1939-1940'. Their names and the words 'Here on this painted glass when life has been subdued your love shall live and be renewed' are at the foot of one of Easton's windows – 'AND THEN THE LOVER'.

In the grounds of the Chapel and looking towards it, is a bronze statue by K. Scott of a boy with arm raised to draw attention, and on the stone plinth are the words, HERE AM I. SEND ME. Presumably meant to demonstrate the patriotism of the 1914 period, the extreme youth of the figure makes it almost a protest for peace.

AVALRY

The Cavalry Memorial in Hyde Park, not far from Hyde Park Corner, has a magnificent bronze by Adrian Jones, of a mounted St. George, with sword aloft, triumphing over the dragon. The figure is on a stone plinth with a bronze frieze depicting imperial cavalry, and the inscription on the plinth reads,

ERECTED BY THE CAVALRY OF THE EMPIRE
IN MEMORY OF COMRADES WHO
GAVE THEIR LIVES IN THE WAR 1914–1919.

ALSO IN THE WAR 1939-1945
AND ON ACTIVE SERVICE THEREAFTER.

The memorial has a granite base, and there is a wall of the same material behind the central figure. On this wall, on bronze plates, are listed the various cavalry regiments of the Empire in the Great War, from Britain, India, Australia, Canada, New Zealand and South Africa. Also on the tablets are the names French, Haig, Allenby and Robertson, and it was the first named, Field Marshal Lord Ypres, who unveiled the memorial on 22 May 1924, on its original site at Stanhope Gate.

ERECTED
BY THE
CAVALRY OF THE EMPIRE
IN MEMORY OF
COMRADES,
WHO GAVE THEIR LIVES
IN THE WAR
1914 1919
ALSO
IN THE WAR

GLASGOW

Glasgow's war memorial stands in the centre of the city, in George Square, with the City Chambers in the background. A massive Cenotaph and Stone of Remembrance flanked by two imposing lions, the memorial is the work of architect Sir John Burnet and sculptor Ernest Gillick.

The unveiling was performed by Field Marshal Earl Haig on Saturday, 31 May 1924 when *The Last Post*, a *Lament* and *The Reveille* were played by the buglers and pipers of the 1st Battalion Highland Light Infantry (the City of Glasgow regiment).

The inscriptions, since amended to include the 1939–1945 war, were, on the front,

PRO PATRIA 1914-1919
TO THE IMMORTAL HONOUR OF THE OFFICERS,
NON-COMMISSIONED OFFICERS AND MEN OF GLASGOW
WHO FELL IN THE GREAT WAR, THIS MEMORIAL
IS DEDICATED IN PROUD AND GRATEFUL RECOGNITION
BY THE CITY OF GLASGOW.

on the north side,

THESE DIED IN WAR THAT WE AT PEACE MIGHT LIVE
THESE GAVE THEIR BEST SO WE OUR BEST SHOULD GIVE.

on the south side,

GREATER LOVE HATH NO MAN THAN THIS
THAT A MAN LAY DOWN HIS LIFE FOR HIS FRIENDS.

and on the back, interestingly,

PRO PATRIA 1914–1919
TOTAL OF HIS MAJESTY'S FORCES ENGAGED AT HOME
AND ABROAD 8,654,465. OF THIS NUMBER THE
CITY OF GLASGOW RAISED OVER 200,000.

MANCHESTER

The Manchester war memorial in St. Peter's Square was designed by Sir Edwin Lutyens and has many of the features characteristic of his work.

Of Portland stone, the memorial covers an area of about 93 foot by 53 foot and stands on the site of the foundations of St. Peter's Church.

A central pylon, thirty-two feet high, is surmounted by a carved bier on which is laid to rest the body of a soldier, covered by his greatcoat and with equipment at his side and feet. On the sides of the pylon are carved the Arms of Manchester and on the ends are swords and imperial crowns. Under one crown is the inscription,

O LORD GOD OF OUR FATHERS, KEEP THIS FOR EVER
IN THE IMAGINATION OF THE THOUGHTS OF
THE HEART OF THY PEOPLE.

and under the other

TO THE HONOURED MEMORY OF THOSE WHO
GAVE THEIR LIVES FOR THEIR COUNTRY.

Flanking the pylon are two obelisks, 23 foot in height, on which are carved the world war dates, and in front is the Great War Stone, 12 foot in length and on which are the words THEIR NAME LIVETH FOR EVERMORE. The stone was a replica of those erected in British cemeteries abroad.

Before the site of the memorial had finally been chosen there had been a great deal of discussion and controversy. A letter dated 11 April 1923 from the British Legion in Manchester had come down emphatically in favour of Albert Square as the site, and the permission of King George V was sought for the removal of the Prince Albert Memorial to a public park. The king granted permission but bodies such as the Manchester Society of Architects, the Manchester Art Federation and the Royal Manchester Institute all expressed opposition to the scheme and so St. Peter's Square was finally chosen. Council minutes show that the City Architect's estimate for the removal and re-erection of the Albert Memorial and other statues in Albert Square was £8,400, an enormous sum, and this may possibly have influenced the final decision.

The memorial was unveiled on 12 July 1924, by the Earl of Derby, assisted by Mrs. Bingle of Ardwick, Manchester, whose three sons were killed in action in France. The dedication of the memorial was by the Dean of Manchester, the Very Reverend J.G. McCormick.

PAISLEY

The Paisley War Memorial unveiled in the town centre to commemorate the 1,953 dead of the First World War, is one of the most impressive. This perhaps is not surprising since the architect, Sir Robert Lorimer, and the sculptress, Alice Meredith-Williams, were each chosen to play a leading part in the development of the Scottish National War Memorial at Edinburgh Castle.

The main feature of the Paisley memorial is a large bronze group of four soldiers of the First World War around the mounted figure of a medieval knight. The soldiers look tired and wet, their heads are down and their collars up, and two are wearing waterproof capes. The knight and the horse, on the other hand, seem alert and ready for battle and the pennant streaming back from the lance bears the cross of St. Andrew. It seems that tradition and history and love of country is what is urging on the tired infantrymen.

The group is on a twenty-five foot high granite pillar with a forty-five foot square platform of Westmorland granite, finished on three sides by a low wall. On the front of the pillar, carved in relief, is a sword of the old Scottish type, the Paisley coat of arms, and shields bearing the St. Andrew's Cross and St. George's Cross.

With the carved inscription referring to the 1914–18 war is a similar one for the 1939–45 period, one difference in style being the reference to the 'MEN AND WOMEN OF THIS BURGH' who gave their lives, compared with the 'MEN OF PAISLEY' originally commemorated.

Bronze plaques list the battle honours of both wars, the Second World War one, for example, including the Battle of Britain, the Far East and Normandy.

The original Town Council motion to erect a memorial was approved as early as 10 September 1918 but a location was not chosen until 1923. At Paisley Cross, on Sunday, 27 July 1924, 20,000 people attended the unveiling performed by Mrs McNab, described as a working class widow who had lost three sons in the war.

LACKBURN

Blackburn's war memorial is situated in a Memorial Garden within Corporation Park on Preston New Road. Figures quoted in 1923 War Memorial Committee minutes suggested that the garden would cost about £2,500 and statuary about £2,000. These figures, in fact, represented only some ten per cent of the money raised at the time, the much larger balance being for an extension to the local Royal Infirmary.

The sculptor chosen by the committee was Sir Bertram MacKennal whose statue of Queen Victoria already existed in the town. His completed work featured a bronze group on a base of Stancliffe stone from Darley Dale with a simple inscription IN REMEMBRANCE 1914–1918, to which has since been added 1939–1945 and 1982, for the Falklands war.

His design also included a fountain to either side of the central base but these features are no longer functioning and, unfortunately, some years ago the bronze lions' heads which were part of the design were stolen from the stonework. It is hoped to address these problems in the near future at the time of a proposed renovation of the park.

MacKennal's main bronze group represents 'the son, returning war-worn after the conflict, received by the Motherland, supported by her, and led to peace'.

The symbolism of this beautiful statue must have added even greater poignancy to the ceremony of unveiling on 2 August 1924, which was carried out by Mrs. Brown, who had lost four sons in the war, and who was assisted by Mrs. Gregory, Mrs Longworth, Mrs. Lowther and Mrs. Taylor, each of whom had lost three sons.

TO THE GLORIOUS MEMORY OF ALL RANKS
THE CAMERONIANS (SCOTTISH RIFLES) WHO,
TO UPHOLD LIBERTY AND JUSTICE IN THE WORLD,
LAID DOWN THEIR LIVES IN THE TWO WORLD WARS
1914 - 1918 AND 1939 - 1945.

THE 6/7ᵗʰ BATTALION, CAMERONIANS (SCOTTISH RIFLES)
WAS DISBANDED ON THE 31ˢᵗ MARCH 1967
THE 1ˢᵗ REGULAR BATTALION ON THE 14ᵗʰ MAY 1968
THUS ENDING THE REGIMENT'S LONG MILITARY ASSOCIATION
WITH THE CITY OF GLASGOW

THIS PLAQUE WAS UNVEILED BY
THE LORD PROVOST OF GLASGOW
THE RT. HON. JOHN JOHNSTON

The Cenotaph in Whitehall, commemorating the British Dead of both World Wars and subsequent wars.

The Royal party's wreaths at the Cenotaph.

The memorial window to three sons of the Huntriss family who lived at Mattersey Hall during the First World War.

An individual memorial at the chapel in Oundle School, dedicated to three members of the Shepley family, who all gave their lives during 1939-1940.

One of the stained-glass windows situated between the main Chapel and the War Memorial Chapel at Rugby School. It depicts an officer on horseback giving encouragement to his troops.

The memorial to the dead of the First World War at Winchester College, recognised in 1924 as one of the finest memorials in the country.

The art gallery in Stockport, featuring the inside of the building. The Memorial Hall has panels of white marble showing the names of 2,200 dead of the First World War.

Photograph courtesy Andy Firth

The striking bronzes of the Guards Division Memorial, erected in 1926 on the St James's Park side of Horse Guards Parade.

Northampton's Town and County War Memorial to the dead of the First World War. The Stone of Remembrance, flanked by twin obelisks adorned with union and service flags, was unveiled by General Lord Horne on 11 November 1926, the eighth anniversary of the Armistice.

A fine stained glass window at the Rolls Royce factory in Derby. It was here that the Merlin engines for Spitfire and Lancaster aircraft were made. Situated above the staircase, the window depicts the figure of a young RAF fighter pilot, standing on the hub of a propeller and looking down on the roofs of the Derby factory.

In memory of ADMIRAL SIR BERTRAM RAMSAY killed in action 1945 who commanded the seaborne forces at Dunkirk 1940

and Normandy 1944 here are remembered also those under his command who were killed during these operations

Two memorial windows to Admiral Ramsay, commander of the seaborne forces at Dunkirk in 1940 and Normandy in 1944. He was killed in action in 1945.

THE STRONGEST LINK

I FEAR NO MAN

Two of the many stained-glass windows in St George's Chapel, Biggin Hill.

Four of the striking stained glass windows at St George's Chapel, Biggin Hill, the most famous station of the Battle of Britain. These four were installed in 1985 to commemorate the ground services of the RAF. In the corner of the 'Ground Control' window are shown three Military Medals, awarded to three WAAF members for bravery during 1940.

Statue at the entrance to the Royal Marines Museum, Southsea.

Air Forces Memorial, Runnymede.

An impressive stained glass Memorial Window, at the Falkland Islands Memorial Chapel at Pangbourne College, in Berkshire. It depicts the Falkland Islands, surrounded by the stormy Atlantic Ocean.

$\mathscr{C}$AMERONIANS

The superb bronze group of the Cameronians' memorial near the Art Gallery in Kelvingrove Park, Glasgow, would perhaps not appeal to those who prefer such memorials to be pacific or compromising in nature. Between a machine gunner and a fallen comrade an infantryman charges forward, his face set with determination, and the effect is an uncomplicated tribute to the basic military virtues of courage and self-sacrifice.

The sculptor of this 1924 work was P. Lindsey Clark and on the stone base is the following inscription,

> TO THE GLORIOUS MEMORY OF ALL RANKS THE
> CAMERONIANS (SCOTTISH RIFLES) WHO, TO UPHOLD
> LIBERTY AND JUSTICE IN THE WORLD, LAID DOWN THEIR
> LIVES IN THE TWO WORLD WARS.

Also inscribed are the lines,

> O VALIANT HEARTS, WHO TO YOUR GLORY CAME
> THROUGH DUST OF CONFLICT AND THRO' BATTLE FLAME,
> TRANQUIL YOU LIE, YOUR KNIGHTLY VIRTUE PROVED,
> YOUR MEMORY HALLOWED IN THE LAND YOU LOVED.

On the back of this memorial are the battle honours of the regiment in the two wars. Under 1914-1918 are listed Mons, Somme, Loos, Hindenburg Line, Gallipoli, Marne, Neuve Chapelle, Ypres, Macedonia and Palestine, while under 1939-1945 are Rhineland, North West Europe, Anzio, Chindits, Scheldt, Sicily, Italy and Burma.

WINCHESTER COLLEGE

Of all the many school memorials to the dead of the First World War, that at Winchester College, in the form of a beautiful cloister designed by Sir Herbert Baker, the architect of the Bank of England, was immediately recognised in 1924 as one of the finest memorials in the country. Kipling described it as 'incomparably the best of all War Memorials'.

The arches round the central Garth are rounded and resting on pairs of simple pillars. The inner walls are faced with local flint and although Portland stone is used for most of the stonework the name tablets on the inner walls are made of Derbyshire Hopton-Wood stone, the tiles of the roof are of Purbeck stone and the paths which intersect the Garth are set with old London paving-stone. Where the paths meet in the centre is a cross protected by two crusader figures, this monument being the work of Alfred Turner.

On the tablets are inscribed the names of five hundred Wykehamists who fell in the war. There are sixteen tablets grouped in pairs, each being linked by a stone recording the great battles of the war. The names of those commemorated are listed by the year in which they came to Winchester and their rank, regiment and place of death are also recorded.

For example, the name of the Prime Minister's son, Raymond Asquith, is listed under 1892 when he came to the college, and he was killed at Trones Wood when a Lieutenant in the Grenadier Guards.

In addition to the name tablets, the Cloister is decorated by the arms and badges of many regiments and allied countries, amongst other carvings, and at each of the four corners is a dome dedicated to the three great Dominions and to India. A long inscription of stone letters runs right round the Cloister in a continuous band nine foot from the ground and reads,

THANKS BE TO GOD FOR THE SERVICE OF THE FIVE
HUNDRED WYKEHAMISTS WHO WERE FOUND FAITHFUL
UNTO DEATH AMID THE MANIFOLD CHANCES OF THE

GREAT WAR. IN THE DAY OF BATTLE THEY FORGAT NOT
GOD, WHO CREATED THEM TO DO HIS WILL, NOR THEIR
COUNTRY, THE STRONGHOLD OF FREEDOM, NOR THEIR
SCHOOL, THE MOTHER OF GODLINESS AND DISCIPLINE.
STRONG IN THIS THREEFOLD FAITH THEY WENT FORTH
FROM HOME AND KINDRED TO THE BATTLEFIELDS OF THE
WORLD, AND TREADING THE PATH OF DUTY AND SACRIFICE
LAID DOWN THEIR LIVES FOR MANKIND.
THOU THEREFORE, FOR WHOM THEY DIED, SEEK
NOT THINE OWN, BUT SERVE AS THEY SERVED,
AND IN PEACE OR IN WAR BEAR THYSELF EVER
AS CHRIST'S SOLDIER, GENTLE IN ALL THINGS,
VALIANT IN ACTION, STEADFAST IN ADVERSITY.

As well as the building of the War Cloister, the memorial fund of the college provided for a new stone altar in the chapel, the reconstruction of the reredos, four memorial volumes, and the full provision of any assistance needed during the whole of their school life for sons of Wykehamists who lost their lives in the War.

The names of the Second World War dead are on plaques on the cloister pillars, and, listed again by their college year, face the names of those of the Great War. The main inscription is,

HERE IN EQUAL HONOUR FACING THE NAMES OF THE
FALLEN IN THE FIRST WORLD WAR ARE INSCRIBED THOSE
OF THE TWO HUNDRED AND SEVENTY WYKEHAMISTS WHO
DIED SERVING IN THE SAME FAITH. 1939 – 1945.

IF OUR TIME BE COME, LET US DIE
MANFULLY FOR OUR BRETHREN, AND
LET US NOT STAIN OUR HONOUR.

The War Cloister is in close proximity to the Boer War Gate commemorating the thirty-two dead of the South Africa campaign 1899–1902. Their names are recorded on a tablet inside the gate, as well as on a Roll placed in a jar along with some coins and a copy of *The Times* of 9 October 1902 and built into the lower stonework. The gate's architect was Frank L. Pearson of London.

Between the gate and the cloister are plaques, commemorating those killed in Palestine, Malaya and Northern Ireland since 1945.

LLANDAFF

On the green above Llandaff Cathedral, Cardiff, is the war memorial to the First World War dead of the Parish and of the Cathedral School. It was unveiled by the Earl of Plymouth, the Lord Lieutenant, on 11 October 1924, in the presence of over 5,000 people.

The memorial, originally entitled 'Departure', has three outstanding bronze figures by Llandaff sculptor Goscombe John, who was also responsible for a number of works within the cathedral, and the nearby figure of Archdeacon Buckley. The centre of the memorial's three figures, a female robed form representing Llandaff, has one arm raised in blessing whilst holding a shield in the other. On the face of the shield is traced a Cross growing out of the oak, or Christianity superseding Druidism.

The two flanking figures are of a schoolboy in shorts and rugby boots and with a rifle slung over his shoulder, and of a workman, perhaps a miner, with sleeves rolled up and with a rifle by his side.

On the plinth beneath the central figure is the inscription,

LLANDAFF REMEMBERS HER OWN SONS AND THOSE
OF THE CATHEDRAL SCHOOL WHO GAVE THEIR
LIVES IN THE GREAT WAR

and, recently added,

AND IN THE SECOND WORLD WAR.

On the base are the words,

NON SIBI SED PATRIAE.
(not for self but for country)

Beneath the workman figure are inscribed the names of fifty-seven parishioners, fifty-six men and one woman, Edith Mary Tonkin VAD, while under the schoolboy are listed a similar number of names, fifty-four, from the Cathedral School.

For the boys of the school it was necessary to walk slowly and with cap off if passing in front of the memorial, while it was permissible to run or wear a cap if using the road behind it.

The memorial is a particularly beautiful one, with its fine sculpture and its situation between the school and cathedral, looking out across the attractive green.

St Anne's

St Anne's War Memorial is unusual in that it was the gift of one man, Lord Ashton, the funds raised for memorial purposes by the community being dedicated to a War Memorial Hospital. The site for the monument was Ashton Gardens, off Clifton Drive, and the sculptor chosen was Walter Marsden, an ex-serviceman who was a native of Accrington but practising in London. He was subsequently responsible for the sculpture on the Bolton memorial, and his other memorial work included that at Bude and Heywood.

The monument is notable for the quality of the three bronze figures by Marsden and by equally fine bronze panels showing scenes such as a soldier saying farewell to his wife and child, another receiving medical treatment and an officer directing a stretcher party and a file of wounded and blinded men.

IN MEMORY OF THOSE WHO FELL 1914–1918

One of the three bronze figures is of a classically robed female with arms outstretched to the sky, supported by a grey granite column forty foot high. On the column's pedestal are two further bronzes. One is of a soldier, seated but alert, with his hand lifting his rifle, and in fact, the artist meant it to represent the warning, 'They're coming again!'

The other is of a mother with a child on her knee and the artist wished to convey that she had just been told of her husband's death and in her shock barely noticed the child's pleadings.

The outstanding work by Marsden was certainly recognised and appreciated at the time of the memorial's unveiling, on 12 October 1924, before a crowd of 15,000 people. The town's mayor, Alderman C.F. Critchley, performed the ceremony, assisted by nine children of war widows, who unveiled sculptures and panels.

The names of the 170 dead were listed on panels on the base of the monument and, subsequently, panels to the 128 dead of the Second World War, and one killed in a later conflict, have been fitted at a higher level on the column.

GREENOCK

The Greenock memorial is sited in Well Park, a high position overlooking the Firth of Clyde, and the War Memorial Booklet published for the unveiling in October 1924 makes the point that 'the sea that flows by Greenock's doors is the very fount of her existence and the foundation of her prosperity'.

The booklet lists the names of the men from the town who gave their lives in the Great War, and who are commemorated by the memorial. There were over 1,500 dead in all, over 400 of whom were Argyll and Sutherland Highlanders.

The architects for the work, Messrs Wright and Wylie of Glasgow, and the sculptor, Alexander Proudfoot of Glasgow, incorporated many unusual features in keeping with Greenock's early history and maritime tradition.

The granite structure consists of a high base on a broad platform, surmounted by a tall obelisk. At the base of the obelisk is the prow of a Viking ship on which is the bronze winged figure of 'Victory' holding aloft a laurel wreath. High up on the face of the obelisk is carved a Celtic cross against which is a two-handed Scottish sword, and there are many other Celtic ornaments carved on the memorial with animal forms being freely used.

To illustrate the history of Scottish shipbuilding, bronze chain palls bear the cross of St. Andrew while nailheads carry the Scottish lion.

An inscription on the base now reads,

AD MAJOREM DEI GLORIAM
AND IN GRATEFUL REMEMBRANCE OF THE MEN OF
GREENOCK WHO GAVE THEIR LIVES IN THE GREAT WAR
AND IN THE 1939–1945 WAR.

Around the memorial is a park with lawns, flower beds and a clear view of the firth and its northern shore.

ROYAL NAVY, PORTSMOUTH

D uring the First World War, the Royal Navy and the navies of the Dominions lost some 48,000 men of whom no fewer than 25,563 were lost or buried at sea and were not recorded in any cemetery or on any battlefield.

In 1920 the Admiralty appointed a Committee to report on the most suitable form and position for a memorial to these men, and as a result of its recommendations three identical monuments, designed by Sir Robert Lorimer, were erected at the three home ports which were the manning ports of the Royal Navy; at Plymouth on the Hoe, at Portsmouth on Southsea Common and at Chatham at the 'Great Lines'.

Each memorial is in the form of an obelisk supported at the four corners by buttresses and each buttress carries a sculptured figure of a lion couchant, looking outwards.

On the base and the buttresses are bronze panels bearing the names of the dead who belonged to the port in question, and on the four faces of the memorial are large bronze panels listing the general actions at sea, Heligoland, Coronel, Falkland Islands, Dogger Bank and Jutland; single ship actions; actions with enemy land forces; and, on the fourth face, the inscription

IN HONOUR OF THE NAVY AND TO THE ABIDING MEMORY
OF THOSE RANKS AND RATINGS OF THIS PORT WHO LAID
DOWN THEIR LIVES IN THE DEFENCE OF THE EMPIRE
AND HAVE NO OTHER GRAVE THAN THE SEA.

Above the base, a column of Portland stone about 100 foot high is crowned by a large copper sphere supported by figures representing the four winds. About a third of the way up the column is carved the badge of the Royal Navy and near the top the prows of four ships are carved in stone.

The memorial at Southsea Common, to over 9,700 men of the Portsmouth Port Division who were lost at sea, was the last of the three to be unveiled, the Duke of York performing the ceremony on Wednesday, 15 October 1924. The naval authorities provided accommodation for 10,000 ticket holders to attend the unveiling but, in all, a crowd of easily three times that number was drawn to the spot.

The memorial at Plymouth, to over 7,000 men, is on the north side of the famous Hoe, between the Armada Memorial and the Drake Statue. It was unveiled on 29 July 1924, by Prince George again in the presence of a vast crowd of some 25,000.

After the Second World War the memorials were much enlarged to accommodate the names of those lost between 1939–45, in general twice the numbers of the first war, a reflection of the greater emphasis on naval activity in the later period.

The architect for the extensions was Sir Edward Maufe and the sculptor Sir Charles Wheeler.

At Portsmouth, a wall to the landward side of the original obelisk, and at a lower level, is inset with fifty-eight bronze name panels. In front of the wall is a garden with lawns, flower beds and paving, and at each end broad steps lead up through a Register Pavilion to the obelisk and the Esplanade. At intervals there are fine stone statues by Wheeler, mostly of naval personnel, and the whole addition blends perfectly with, and indeed enhances, the original.

ERBY

In its account of the unveiling ceremony of the Derby war memorial to some 2,000 dead, *The Derbyshire Advertiser* described the memorial itself, designed by the sculptor Arthur G. Walker, as follows:

> 'The Monument is a beautiful conception in bronze and stone, typifying the widowed mother, grief stricken but proud and courageous, holding her fatherless boy, with the Cross in the background.'

The notes in the souvenir booklet issued at the time of the ceremony put a slightly different interpretation on the work,

> 'So here the whole vision is embodied in a typical English mother, bowed with her sorrow but not broken-hearted, for she is not alone in her grief, she is but one of a countless number of similar sufferers and she is thrilled with the glory of the great sacrifice of her son – cherishing the younger boy, who while clinging to his mother in perfect confidence, looks out and reaches out... .'

Either interpretation would be logical, and perhaps that in the booklet should be taken as the official one, but in that case the female figure does appear to be rather young.

The memorial was unveiled by Alderman Ling in the Market Place on Armistice Day, Tuesday, 11 November 1924, and dedicated by the Bishop of Derby. Amongst the wreaths laid was one from the mother of the late Private Rivers, Derby's only Great War VC.

In addition to building the monument, the city also endowed a hospital bed at the local infirmary in memory of the dead, and a cheque for £1,000 was handed over for that purpose during the ceremony.

The memorial, to its advantage, is now in a pedestrianised area of the city, with flower beds to either side of the base on which is now inscribed,

FOR FAITH AND HOME AND RIGHTEOUSNESS
WORLD WAR 1939 – 1945.

On the back are the words,

IN HONOUR OF THOSE WHO HAVE FALLEN IN
CONFLICT SINCE 1945.

and   IN HONOUR OF THOSE CIVILIANS WHO
LOST THEIR LIVES IN WAR.

KEIGHLEY

Keighley's thirty-five foot high memorial with its supporting bronze figures of a soldier and a sailor, and surmounted by a bronze figure of Victory, was designed by Henry C. Fehr who had earlier been responsible for the Leeds memorial.

On 7 December 1924, over 20,000 people attended the unveiling by Lieutenant-General Sir Charles Harington, who was GOC Northern Command. The memorial commemorated some 900 men of the town, and children of those who had fallen were allowed to stand at the front of the huge crowd so that they could more easily lay wreaths at the end of the ceremony.

The mayor of Poix-du-Nord, Keighley's adopted French town, attended and presented a bronze laurel wreath which remained at the base of the memorial for many years before apparently disappearing in the 1970s.

Other changes since the unveiling are the loss of the blade of the soldier's bayonet, sadly a not uncommon form of vandalism, the addition of Second World War dates and references to it, and the addition in Millennium Year 2000 of a metal plaque, as a tribute to the dead from the Royal British Legion and the Duke of Wellington's Regimental Association.

The Keighley memorial is a most impressive one, on a prominent corner site, and the bronzes are particularly fine.

EDWARD HORNER

The Church of St. Andrew in the village of Mells in Somerset has, to the left of the chancel, what used to be the Lady Chapel, but later became the Horner Chapel, containing the Horner family vault, and marble plaques to some of those buried below.

In the centre of the chapel, and dominating it, is a bronze equestrian statue of Edward Horner, the last direct male heir to the Horner Estate. A Lieutenant in the 18th Hussars, he died of wounds at Noyelles on 21 November 1917, in the Battle of Cambrai.

His only brother had died before the war, and in September 1916 his sister, who eventually inherited the family estate, was widowed when her husband, Raymond Asquith, son of the Prime Minister, was killed whilst serving as a lieutenant in the Grenadier Guards.

The statue of Edward Horner is the work of Sir Alfred Munnings and is said to be the first horse sculpture by this famous painter of horses. As a result of this work he was asked by the Jockey Club Members to make a statue of Brown Jack for the Epsom course.

The base of the memorial at Mells was designed by Sir Edwin Lutyens, a friend of the family, and set into it is the cross which marked Horner's grave in France.

Also in the chapel is the cross which marked the grave in France of Raymond Asquith. Elsewhere, on the south wall of the church, is a memorial to him, with lettering by Eric Gill and a bronze wreath above by Lutyens.

A further connection of the church with the First World War is the grave in the churchyard of the famous war poet Siegfried Sassoon. His last wish was to be buried near Ronald Knox, the priest and scholar who for some years lived at the Manor nearby.

Recently, a plan by the parish church council has caused considerable controversy. The proposal is to move the equestrian memorial of Edward Horner from the Horner Chapel to a new position within the church. Such suggestions for change in relation to war memorials are invariably less than popularly received.

Arguments in favour of the status quo include the

sentiment that after eighty years the memorial should not be subject to disturbance for any reason. Secondly, the appropriate position for a Horner statue is arguably in the Horner Chapel.

On the other hand, setting aside the council's perceived need for a more flexible use of their church in times of decreasing attendances, and concentrating only on the war memorial aspects of the debate, the statue is certainly very cramped in its present position. It was originally intended to place the memorial under the bell tower where various other monuments are to be found, but the floor was not sufficiently strong and so its present position was chosen, virtually out of necessity.

The Horner Chapel measures approximately eighteen foot by thirteen foot while the memorial's plinth measures just over five foot by three-and-a-half foot. It is certainly difficult to stand back and admire the statue in comfort at present. It would without doubt be seen to greater advantage in the new proposed position in the church, but of course at the cost of continuity, if that should be considered an overriding factor.

$\mathscr{D}$UNDEE

A t a public meeting held in Dundee as early as January 1919 it was unanimously decided to erect a war memorial to commemorate over four thousand fallen of the 30,000 Dundee men who served in the war. Difficulties over fund-raising and indecision about the site and type of memorial required, however, led to considerable delay, and it was not until September 1923 that the War Memorial Committee, with some £12,000 in hand, accepted a tender from R. Pert & Son, Montrose, to construct a monument to the design of the architect Thomas Braddock.

Braddock's design had been selected after a competition held under the auspices of the R.I.B.A., and Sir Robert Lorimer of Edinburgh had been the assessor. Described as 'an arresting monolith' the winning design was to be built of granite with a bronze brazier surmounting it, and the site chosen was the Law, a 570 foot hill which forms the backdrop to the City. The choice of site was by no means universally approved and amongst the criticism it was suggested that the memorial would be too inaccessible and that it would destroy the hill's natural appearance.

It had been hoped to use Aberdeen granite for the construction but the tender accepted was for Cornish granite at a price of £7,950, the same contractor's figure for Aberdeen granite being £9,900.

In addition to the monument, separate permanent records of the names of the dead were prepared, one list being shown on panels on an oak stand in the Permanent Gallery of the Albert Institute and another in the form of a book placed in the Town House.

It was hoped to have the memorial unveiled in November 1924 by Earl Haig, but a builders' strike led to considerable delay in the bronze work for the brazier and the door of the monument, the work being the responsibility of a Cheltenham firm.

Eventually, General Sir Ian Hamilton unveiled the complete monument on Saturday, 16 May 1925. Because of the restricted nature of the site, accommodation on the Law was provided only for the platform party, aged relatives of the fallen, limbless soldiers, representatives of the various regiments, and members of the Town Council and War Memorial Committee, but loudspeakers were erected so that the crowds further down the hill could follow the service and speeches.

A guard of honour was provided by the 4th/5th Black Watch and, as the monument was unveiled, pipers played *Lochaber No More*.

Sir Ian Hamilton's speech was rather more direct than many such speeches were at the time. He was forthright about the widespread unemployment of former soldiers and urged the government to start work of national importance immediately to reduce such unemployment. He also had no kind word for scientists. His speech included the following words,

> 'The luminous mass of Cornish granite breaks from the Imperial colours in which it was swathed and stands four-square upon the Law where there is no reason it should not endure till the scientists who invented poison gas carry out their principles to a logical conclusion and explode their own planet.'

At the conclusion of the ceremony, Sir Ian's programme included visits to *Dunalistair*, the memorial holiday home established by the Black Watch at Broughty Ferry, and to houses at Barnhill erected by the Veterans' Garden City Association for the housing of disabled men.

An interesting newspaper item before the unveiling ceremony describes proceedings at a meeting of the Dundee Magistrates, when a letter was submitted from the Secretary of the Shop Assistants' Union asking the Magistrates to recommend the closing of shops for three or four hours on the afternoon of Saturday, 16 May.

Baillie Smith is reported as saying 'Ridiculous nonsense; that's the only day we get any money'. Baillie Gillies thought that the Magistrates could make the recommendation and let the shopkeepers do what they wished. In the event it seems that Smith misjudged the mood of the city as on the day of the ceremony a majority of shops were closed.

Today the memorial can be seen not only from most parts of the city but also from the surrounding countryside. To the inscription referring to 'The Great War 1914–1918' has been added a similar one to 'The World War 1939–1945'. The memorial is well preserved and imposing, with the immediate surface having been improved in recent years, and the views from the Law over the city to the Tay estuary are spectacular.

LEICESTER

The Leicester war memorial was not unveiled until 4 July 1925, and at the time of the ceremony only £16,000 had been raised towards the target of £25,000. The editorial comment in the Leicester Advertiser at that time was frank in its criticism,

'It is indeed a disgrace, that nearly seven years after the cessation of hostilities we should be touting around to get money to pay for what should have been bought and paid for at least five years ago. It could have been obtained then quite easily, but dilatoriness on the part of those who had control and a lack of tact in dealing with the public, caused the whole thing to fall flat. I attended all the public meetings called (none too early) to decide upon a suitable memorial and the impression I got, in common with others, was of an attempt to keep the decision entirely in a few hands.

The public does not like that sort of thing, and it has shown its disapproval by not throwing itself into the scheme with enthusiasm. The result is that Leicester, though some eight times as big as Loughborough, has had a struggle to raise as much money as Loughborough has already spent.'

However, the article went on to praise the scheme which had been accepted and to express determination that the balance of the money required would be found.

The memorial, an Arch of Remembrance designed by Sir Edwin Lutyens, was erected in Victoria Park to the memory of those of the City and County who died. Made of Portland Stone, it enshrines flags within the arch and on the front facing the avenue from London Road are the words,

REMEMBER IN GRATITUDE TWELVE THOUSAND MEN OF
THIS CITY AND COUNTY WHO FOUGHT AND DIED FOR
FREEDOM. REMEMBER ALL WHO SERVED AND STROVE
AND THOSE WHO PATIENTLY ENDURED.

The unveiling was performed by Mrs. Elizabeth Ann Butler a widow, aged sixty-nine, assisted by Mrs. Annie Elizabeth Glover, also a widow, aged fifty-three. Mrs. Butler had lost four sons in the war and had two others wounded. At the outbreak of the war she had no fewer than eleven sons and six daughters living, and eight of the sons served in the army.

Mrs. Glover was the mother of eight sons and five daughters and three of her sons were killed in action, as well as two nephews and two brothers-in-law.

The Bishop of Peterborough dedicated the memorial and a crowd of some 30,000 attended the service and the unveiling.

BIRMINGHAM

The foundation stone of the Birmingham Hall of Memory was laid by the Prince of Wales on 12 June 1923 and the Hall was opened by Prince Albert of Connaught on 4 July 1925, when it was dedicated by the Bishop of Birmingham. An estimated 30,000 people attended the ceremony.

This Hall is a massive octagonal structure in Roman Doric style, thirty-five foot wide and standing in a garden of flower beds. On a base of Cornish granite, it is of Portland stone with a domed roof. The huge doors are of bronze, and four bronze figures representing the Army, Navy, Air Force and the nation's Women, are on granite pedestals at the corners of the building.

In the interior a sarcophagus-shaped marble shrine supports the glass and bronze casket originally containing one Roll of Honour, the frontispiece of which has a richly coloured and gilt border framing the words,

> THERE WAS NONE THAT GAVE THEM AN ILL WORD,
> FOR THEY FEARED GOD GREATLY. SO THEY PASSED
> OVER, AND ALL THE TRUMPETS SOUNDED FOR
> THEM ON THE OTHER SIDE.

150,000 men and women of Birmingham had served in the war and of those 12,320 were killed and 35,000 wounded. Lists of names to be included in the Roll had remained open for weeks in case of necessary amendment, and the numbers had increased considerably during the latter period.

The casket now contains an additional Roll for the 1939–1945 war and a plaque refers to both wars. Similarly plaques at the entrance to the Hall refer to the dead of 1914–18 and 1939–45.

A stained-glass window showing the Cross faces the main entrance and on the walls are three bas-reliefs illustrating episodes of the war. The first shows men leaving home for the war. The second shows them in the firing line with the inscription,

> AT THE GOING DOWN OF THE SUN AND IN THE
> MORNING WE WILL REMEMBER THEM.

The third shows men returning home, wounded and maimed, with the inscription,

> SEE TO IT THAT THEY SHALL NOT HAVE SUFFERED
> AND DIED IN VAIN.

The artists involved in the work were Albert Toft the sculptor of the bronze statues, Sidney Meteyard the designer of the Roll of Honour, William Bloye the designer of the *bas-reliefs*, R.J. Stubington the designer of the glass work, and the architects S.N. Cooke and W.N. Twist who were both ex-servicemen. Sir Reginald Blomfield had chosen the design after assessing those submitted.

The cost of the Hall was over £60,000, all from public subscription, and excluding the cost of the land which was given by the Corporation.

The Birmingham Hall of Memory is an impressive and appropriate tribute to the thousands of war dead of the city, and in recent years improvements have been made to the immediate area surrounding the building.

Moreover, the Hall is now open to the public, when at one time access had to be sought from the City Hall.

ABERDEEN

lans for Aberdeen's war memorial, despite the scope and complexity of the scheme, were published in great detail as early as August 1919 when the *Aberdeen Daily Journal* explained the proposed lay-out and anticipated financial requirements. In fact, from that time until the scheme's fruition, there was little change to the details published.

The whole development consisted of a Memorial Court or Hall of Remembrance, an extension to the city's art gallery, a large hall and an art museum. The architects were Dr. A. Marshall Mackenzie, who was the architect of the original Art Gallery building, and A.G.R. Mackenzie.

Facing Union Terrace Gardens, the exterior of the Memorial Court was of a concave shape, with six Corinthian pillars on a raised platform, in front of a wall upon which were carved a wreath of laurels, the arms of the city and county, the words TO OUR GLORIOUS DEAD, and the dates 1914–1919 in Roman numerals. The dates 1939–1945 have since been added.

In front, in the centre of the crescent, was a lion modelled by William MacMillan, and on either side of the pillared wall was a handsome pier, each with an entrance door, one to the Memorial Court and one to the new hall and museum. The whole of the striking exterior was built of white granite.

The Memorial Court itself was circular, rising almost eighty foot to the top of a dome above. A hall large enough to accommodate 700 people was designed above an art museum, and other rooms served as extensions to the original art gallery.

The whole scheme cost in the region of £70,000. The site for the buildings cost the Corporation £7,000; £21,000 was subscribed by the public towards the war memorial; of the £12,000 contributed to the art gallery extensions, the sum of £7,000 came from the Clark Trustees; and Lord and Lady Cowdray generously offered to provide the Hall and Art Museum at a cost of £20,000, together with an organ for the hall.

A marble tablet bearing the sculptured Cowdray coat-of-arms, carried the inscription,

THE COWDRAY HALL AND ART MUSEUM WERE PRESENTED
TO THE CITY BY VISCOUNT AND VISCOUNTESS COWDRAY
FOR THE ADVANCEMENT OF LEARNING AND THE
ENCOURAGEMENT OF ART AND MUSIC AMONG THE
CITIZENS OF ABERDEEN, 1925.

The new buildings were opened by King George V on 29 September, 1925 and the war memorial was dedicated by the Moderators of the Church of

Scotland and United Free Church of Scotland.

The Gordon Highlanders provided the King's guard of honour, and amongst the people to whom the King spoke was Captain Albert Hutcheon, MC, who was blinded leading a company of the 5th Gordon Highlanders.

The Roll of Honour inside the Memorial Court contained 5,042 names – 535 officers, 4,505 other ranks and two women, a nurse and a medical missionary.

Four VCs were listed, Captain James A.O. Brooke of the Gordon Highlanders, Lieutenant Robert G. Combe of the Canadian Light Infantry, Captain Archibald B. Smith of the Royal Naval Reserve, and Brigadier Frederick W. Lumsden of the Royal Marine Artillery, who won not only the VC but the DSO and three bars, believed to be a record for the British army. Captain Brooke was one of three brothers whose names were on the roll, and a brother-in-law also fell. There were several instances of four members of a family being listed and one family lost five sons.

The father of that family, Peter Tocher, formally placed the Roll of Honour in the casket on the shrine of the Memorial Court. He had lost one son, George, on the Menin Road near Ypres in 1915, three sons, Robert, John and James on the Somme in 1916, and one, Peter, after the war, his health undermined by four years as a prisoner of war. All five men were Gordon Highlanders, and their father also joined the regiment despite being fifty years old, but because of his age was not passed for active service.

Within the Memorial Court there are now four Rolls of Honour. In front of a green marble wall on which is the inscription,

THEY GAVE THEIR LIVES FOR THEIR COUNTRY
AND FOR FREEDOM.

and flanked by union and service flags, are the original 1914–1919 Roll for Aberdeen and District, a 1939–1945 Roll for the City of Aberdeen, a 1939–1945 Roll for the Merchant Navy and Fishing Fleets, and a Roll for the City of Aberdeen since 1945.

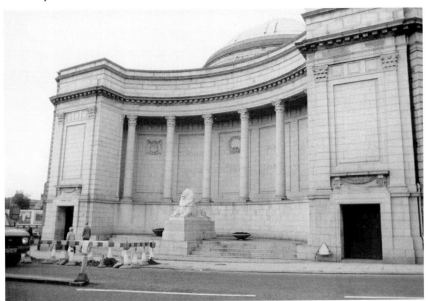

GALASHIELS

The war memorial in the centre of the town of Galashiels, in the Scottish Borders, has several most unusual features.

A massive clock tower has at its base a large bronze plaque bearing the names of the dead of the First World War, and to each side of that a smaller plate with Second World War names.

Above this, carved in stone, is a female figure with head bowed and holding a laurel wreath in each hand, and also in stone, the words,

FOR REMEMBRANCE.

In front of the name plaque is a magnificent bronze equestrian statue on a stone plinth, of a 'Border Reiver' from Gala's earlier history.

Each evening a few bars of the *Braw, Braw Lads* is played in memory of the fallen after the chimes of the clock, and when at dusk the lighting is switched on, the shadows of what appear to be perfect wings are cast on to the female figure on the front of the memorial.

A plaque to one side of the tower refers to the laying of an inscribed stone in the presence of the Prince of Wales on 3 December 1924, and the unveiling ceremony by Field Marshal Earl Haig of Bemersyde on 4 October 1925. The sculptor was Thomas J. Clapperton.

STOCKPORT

Stockport's war memorial is an art gallery of classical appearance, built, at a total cost of £24,000, on the site of the old Stockport Grammar School. At the top of a flight of twenty-three wide steps, the Portland stone building is in an elevated and prominent position at the junction of two main roads. In recent years, unfortunately, road alterations have meant the loss of an attractive flower bed between the traffic and the foot of the steps.

On either side of the steps are walls on which are carved respectively 1914–1918, and 1939–1945. To the sides of the heavy entrance doors are the inscriptions,

THIS FOUNDATION STONE WAS LAID BY HIS WORSHIP
THE MAYOR OF STOCKPORT ALDERMAN CHAS. ROYLE J P
ON SEPTEMBER 15TH 1923.

and

THIS MEMORIAL WAS OPENED BY HIS ROYAL HIGHNESS THE
PRINCE HENRY K.G., G.C.V.O. ON OCTOBER 15TH 1925
HENRY PATTEN, MAYOR.

Inside the building, which was designed by Messrs. Halliday, Agate and Paterson of Manchester, the Memorial Hall itself has panels of white marble containing the names of some 2,200 dead of the First World War, and the same material has been used for a memorial sculpture group by Gilbert Ledward featuring Britannia holding a sword of honour and a laurel wreath of victory, and standing behind a kneeling figure symbolic of the men who fell in the war. At the man's feet lies a dead serpent and he holds a broken sword to signify sacrifice.

After the Second World War, additional marble panels, with the names of the fallen, were built into the wall behind Ledward's work, and in 1983 two more tablets were added with the names of those lost in Korea, Northern Ireland and the Falklands.

On each side of the entrance hall of the building is a small exhibition gallery, and on the first floor is the main gallery, from the entrance to which it is possible to look down into the impressive Memorial Hall or upwards to the dome.

ROYAL ARTILLERY

One of the most powerful of all war memorials is that, unveiled on 18 October 1925 by the Duke of Connaught, at Hyde Park Corner, to the 49,076 First World War dead of the Royal Artillery.

It was designed by Lionel Pearson who also designed the Sandham Memorial at Burghclere, and the sculptor was Charles Sargeant Jagger, whose other war memorial works included that at Hoylake, Portsmouth, Bedford and Paddington, although the Artillery Memorial can be considered his major work.

The memorial is a massive stepped stone base surmounted by an enormous stone howitzer, while on the sides of the base, at a lower level, are bronze statues of artillerymen and stone reliefs of both heavy and horse artillery.

The marvellous bronzes, one on each side of the monument, are of an officer, a driver, a shell carrier, and seen at a low level instead of a conventionally raised one, a dead soldier covered with his greatcoat and with his helmet placed on his chest. Around this figure are inscribed the words,

HERE WAS A ROYAL FELLOWSHIP OF DEATH.

and on the stone below,

BENEATH THIS STONE IS BURIED THE ROLL OF HONOUR OF THOSE WHOSE MEMORY IS PERPETUATED BY THIS MEMORIAL. THEY WILL RETURN NEVER MORE, BUT THEIR GLORY WILL ABIDE FOREVER.

Other inscriptions are of the regimental motto 'UBIQUE', the list of theatres of war, the reference to the 49,076 fatalities, and, subsequently,

THIS PANEL WAS ADDED TO COMMEMORATE THE 29,924 OF ALL RANKS OF THE ROYAL ARTILLERY WHO GAVE THEIR LIVES FOR THEIR KING AND COUNTRY IN ALL PARTS OF THE WORLD DURING THE WAR OF 1939-1945.

THEY DIED WITH THE FAITH THAT THE FUTURE OF ALL MANKIND WOULD BENEFIT BY THEIR SACRIFICE.

QUO FAS ET GLORIA DUCUNT.

ERECTED TO
COMMEMORATE
THE GLORIOUS
HEROES
OF THE
MACHINE GUN
CORPS
WHO FELL IN
THE GREAT
WAR

MCMXIV

MCMXIX

MACHINE GUN CORPS

The Machine Gun Corps Memorial, unveiled by the Duke of Connaught in 1925 at Hyde Park Corner, close to the Royal Artillery Memorial, has as its main feature a bronze figure of David by Derwent Wood. The naked David is holding the slain Goliath's huge sword and an inscription on the stone base of the memorial is,

SAUL HATH SLAIN HIS THOUSANDS BUT DAVID
HIS TENS OF THOUSANDS.

a brutally frank quotation from 1 Samuel, chapter 18, verse 7.

To either side of the figure and at a slightly lower level is a bronze machine gun covered by two laurel wreaths, and on the back of the central pedestal is inscribed a short history of the Corps.

Its Colonel-in-Chief was King George V and it was formed on 14 October 1915, and disbanded finally on 15 July 1922. The Corps served in France, Flanders, Russia, Italy, Egypt, Palestine, Mesopotamia, Salonica, India, Afghanistan, and East Africa. The total number who served was some 11,500 officers and 159,000 other ranks, of whom 1,120 officers and 12,671 other ranks were killed, and 2,881 officers and 45,377 other ranks were wounded, missing or prisoners of war.

HEFFIELD

The Sheffield war memorial, in Barker's Pool in front of the City Hall, was unveiled on Wednesday, 28 October 1925, by Lieutenant-General Sir Charles H. Harington, GOC Northern Command, and dedicated by the Bishop of Sheffield.

The official party, including not only the principals and the Mayor, City Council and officers, but also representatives of the Cutlers' Company and of Sheffield University, assembled at the Town Hall and moved in procession to the Cathedral where a service was conducted by the Vicar of Sheffield, Archdeacon J.R. Derbyshire, and an address was given by the Bishop.

From there the procession moved on to the memorial site where the band of the Queen's Own Yorkshire Dragoons had been playing appropriate selections. During the ceremony itself buglers of the York and Lancashire Regiment sounded *The Last Post* and *Reveille*.

The memorial, by architect C.D. Carus Wilson and sculptor George Alexander, is an unusual one, being a ninety foot high flag-pole at the top of which is a golden crown, while at the foot is a massive, and very ornate base. This beautifully worked base is decorated by the figures of four soldiers with rifles reversed and heads bowed, and by coats of arms representing the Army, Navy, Air Force, City, Yorkshire Dragoons (Queen's Own), Royal Artillery, Royal Engineers, Machine Gun Corps, Tank Corps, York and Lancaster Regiment, Medical Corps, and the Royal Army Service Corps.

TO THE GLORY OF GOD
AND IN MEMORY OF THE
OFFICERS WARRANT OFFICERS
NON COMMISSIONED OFFICERS &
GUARDSMEN OF HIS MAJESTY'S
REGIMENTS OF FOOT GUARDS
WHO GAVE THEIR LIVES FOR THEIR
KING AND COUNTRY DURING THE
GREAT WAR 1914-1918 AND OF THE
OFFICERS WARRANT OFFICERS AND
NON COMMISSIONED OFFICERS AND
MEN OF THE HOUSEHOLD CAVALRY
ROYAL REGIMENT OF ARTILLERY
CORPS OF ROYAL ENGINEERS
ROYAL ARMY SERVICE CORPS ROYAL
ARMY MEDICAL CORPS AND OTHER
UNITS WHO WHILE SERVING WITH
THE GUARDS DIVISION IN FRANCE &
BELGIUM 1915-18 FELL WITH THEM IN
THE FIGHT FOR THE WORLD'S FREEDOM

UARDS DIVISION

The bronzes by Gilbert Ledward are the most striking feature of the Guards Division Memorial designed by H.C. Bradshaw and erected in 1926 on the St. James's Park side of Horse Guards Parade. The stone monolith is itself elegant and impressive but attention is instantly focused on the figures of five life-size guardsmen, each from a different guards regiment, standing in line and facing the parade ground and Whitehall.

Beneath the guardsmen, which were cast from bronze salvaged from captured German guns, are the regimental badges of, respectively, the Grenadier, Scots, Welsh, Irish and Coldstream Guards, in stone relief.

Bronze panels are set into the other three sides of the monument, the scene of artillery in action, on the side facing St. James's Park, being particularly interesting.

The original inscription on the stone of the memorial was by Rudyard Kipling but since has been added,

THIS MEMORIAL ALSO COMMEMORATES ALL
THOSE MEMBERS OF THE HOUSEHOLD DIVISION
WHO DIED IN THE SECOND WORLD WAR AND IN
THE SERVICE OF THEIR COUNTRY SINCE 1918.

HARROW SCHOOL

T he First World War Memorial at Harrow School is the War Memorial Building designed by Sir Herbert Baker, the architect of Winchester's Cloister. The memorial's external architecture closely reflects that of the surrounding buildings of the school.

The main feature of the memorial is the Shrine on the ground floor where the names of over 600 Old Boys and Masters who fell in 1914-18 are carved into the walls, and the roof bosses bear the arms of England, Harrow School and France, to represent the places of birth, education and death of the fallen.

A stone altar at one end has carved above it, in the curved wall of a niche, the inscription,

O VALIANT HEARTS WHO TO YOUR GLORY CAME
THROUGH DUST OF CONFLICT AND THROUGH BATTLE FLAME,
TRANQUIL YOU LIE YOUR KNIGHTLY VIRTUE PROVED,
YOUR MEMORY HALLOWED IN THE LAND YOU LOVED.

On the first floor of the building, one of the rooms is dedicated to the memory of 2nd Lieutenant Alex Fitch of the Royal Garrison Artillery, who died on 18 September 1918, at the age of nineteen. His parents, Sir Cecil and Lady Fitch, gave the room, with its furniture and fittings, and a portrait of their son hangs above the Tudor fireplace. Although the room dates only from 1926, the furniture and fittings are antique, the panelling being Tudor and the floor timbers made from the St. Vincent, a Georgian Warship. The table in the centre of the room is Cromwellian. To quote from the school's own description,

THE ROOM IS HISTORY, ITS INSPIRATION WAS MEMORY,
BUT ITS PURPOSE IS FOR TODAY AND TOMORROW.

In the room are kept copies of the six volumes of the Book of Remembrance of the school. The entries are in order of date of death, and there is a short biography and photograph of each of the fallen.

The Shrine was dedicated by Randall Davidson, the Archbishop of Canterbury, and the War Memorial was opened in 1926 by Mr. Stanley Baldwin, the Prime Minister. Both men were themselves old Harrovians.

On the ground floor of the War Memorial Building there is now an area dedicated to the Harrovians who died in the Second World War. Their names are inscribed on bronze tablets and a circular bronze plaque on the floor indicates the purpose of this shrine.

In the school Chapel, built in 1855, the right hand aisle was erected as a memorial to Old Boys killed in the Crimean War, and the transepts commemorate those who fell in the Boer War.

The Alex Fitch room.

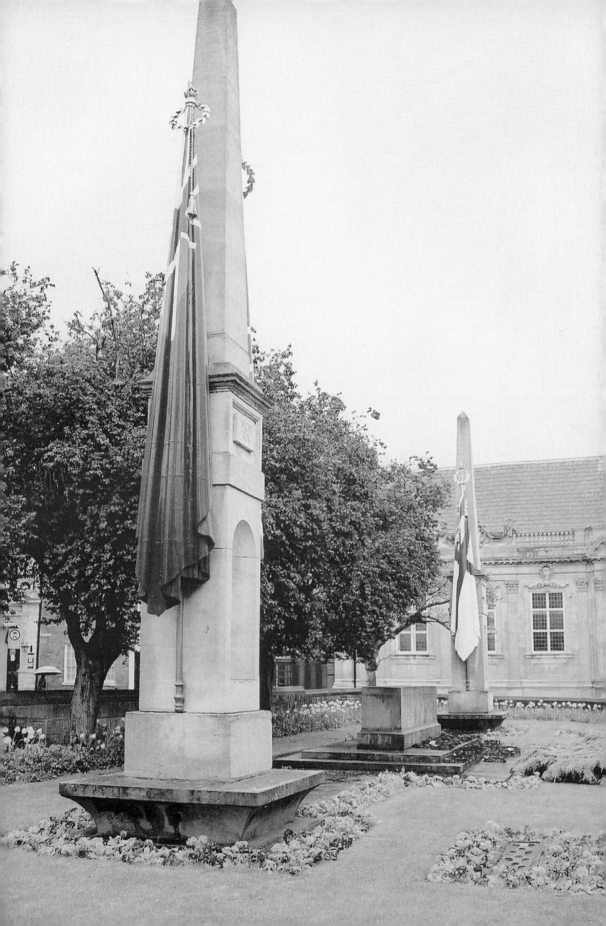

NORTHAMPTON

Northampton's Town and County war memorial to the dead of the First World War was designed by Sir Edwin Lutyens and unveiled by General Lord Horne on 11 November 1926, the eighth anniversary of the Armistice. A few months later the Prince of Wales paid tribute by laying a wreath.

Also now commemorated are the dead of the Second World War.

The memorial, next to All Saints Church, consists of a Stone of Remembrance or Great War Stone, flanked by twin obelisks adorned with union and service flags. The surrounding garden, with stone walls and large metal gates, is well-tended and colourful.

In 1937, a Garden of Remembrance was opened some distance away, in Abington Square, where the main features were a wall recording the names of the dead, and the Mobbs memorial moved from its original site in the Market Place.

The Prince of Wales at the Northampton Memorial, after laying a wreath.

BURNLEY

The Burnley memorial to the dead of the First World War was unveiled in Towneley Park on Sunday, 12 December 1926 by Lord Derby, and dedicated by the Bishop of Burnley the Right Reverend Henry Henn, before a crowd estimated at almost 30,000.

The memorial was designed and sculpted by Walter Gilbert of Birmingham and consists of a twenty foot high central block of Portland stone carved at the top into the figures of three service men, representing the Navy, Army and Air Force.

At the sides of the central feature are two, eight foot high bronze female figures, the one on the left representing a mother laying a wreath and the one on the right representing a wife or sister offering garlands. A poignant detail is the positioning at the mother's feet of her son's cricket bat and ball, and a rosemary bush for remembrance.

To the original inscription on the plinth,

THIS MONUMENT WAS ERECTED IN MEMORY OF
THE MEN OF BURNLEY WHO GAVE THEIR LIVES
FOR THEIR FELLOW-COUNTRYMEN IN
THE GREAT WAR 1914-1918.

MAKE THEM TO BE NUMBERED WITH THY SAINTS
IN GLORY EVERLASTING.

have been added the words,

THE MONUMENT STANDS ALSO IN HONOUR OF
THOSE WHO DIED FOR OUR FREEDOM
1939-1945.

Although the memorial is a beautiful and appropriate one, Towneley Park is certainly some distance from the city centre of Burnley and in the 1960s an association of ex-servicemen raised the necessary finance and erected a new memorial stone in the centre, the unveiling and dedication taking place on 30 October 1966.

$\mathscr{S}$ANDHAM MEMORIAL CHAPEL

In 1915 the controversial artist Stanley Spencer joined the RAMC as an orderly, and shortly afterwards was posted to Macedonia where he ultimately served with the 7th Royal Berkshire Regiment until the end of the war.

In 1922 he started work on designs for a series of mural paintings depicting scenes from his war experiences, and these were seen by his friends Mr. and Mrs. Louis Behrend who undertook to build a chapel to house the finished work.

The chapel was built at Burghclere, near Newbury, between 1923 and 1927, to the designs of another friend of the Behrends, Lionel Pearson who was involved in the design also of the Royal Artillery Memorial.

The chapel was dedicated on 25 March 1927, as the Oratory of All Souls, subsequently becoming known as the Sandham Memorial Chapel in memory of Mrs. Behrend's brother H.W. Sandham who had died in 1919 from illness whilst serving, also, in Macedonia. The chapel was given to the National Trust by the Behrends in 1947 and remains in its ownership today.

The nineteen paintings in the chapel were executed by Spencer between 1927 and 1932. They are, in fact, not murals but in oil on large seamless canvases woven in Belgium. The best known, perhaps, 'The Resurrection of the Soldiers', dominates the chapel, taking up the whole of the east wall opposite the entrance door and behind the altar. This painting alone took the artist nearly a year to complete. As a whole, the cycle emphasises the everyday incidents of army life rather than the horrors of the trenches, and the other eighteen paintings include such mundane scenes as *convoy arriving with wounded, kit inspection, reveille and map-reading.*

$\mathscr{S}$COTTISH NATIONAL WAR MEMORIAL

The idea of a National War Memorial for Scotland was first suggested in 1917 and in due course a committee was appointed with the Prince of Wales as President and the Duke of Atholl as Chairman. Subscriptions were invited from Scots both at home and overseas, the first subscription received, apparently, being one of £500 from a prominent business man, and the second being half-a-crown from an ex-tinker who served with the Black Watch.

The architect chosen was Sir Robert Lorimer, and wherever possible Scottish materials and artists were employed. The selected site was, most appropriately, the Castle Rock in Edinburgh, and the memorial building forms the north side of Crown Square, at the highest part of the Castle and facing the historic and ancient Banqueting Hall. The building incorporates the walls of the former barracks and the style of the detail is characteristic of sixteenth century Scottish architecture.

The memorial is basically rectangular in plan with projections into Crown Square at each end, and with a semi-circular projection on the opposite, or northern side. This apse faces the entrance porch and contains the shrine. Within the shrine the Castle Rock is exposed through the granite floor, and on it is the marble pedestal supporting the wrought steel casket which holds the Rolls of Honour with the names of the 100,000 Scottish dead of the Great War, to which were subsequently added those of the Second World War.

A bronze frieze round the walls of the shrine depicts a procession of Scots service-men and women in uniform, some sixty figures in all, and above there are seven stained-glass windows illustrating the Birth of War (2), the Overthrow of Tyranny (2), the Triumph of the Spirit, Praise, and Peace. Hanging from the vaulted roof, and directly above the casket, is an oak figure of St. Michael, a symbol of the triumph of Good over Evil.

On either side of the entrance porch, and forming the bulk of the building, is the Hall of Honour with bays containing the memorials of the twelve Scottish Regiments, each with a stone table on which rest Books of Remembrance. Also within the Hall are memorials to the various other arms and services, and further stained-glass windows, this time showing scenes of war.

Royal Engineers.

Padres.

The regimental memorials are to the Scots Guards, Royal Scots Greys, Royal Scots, Royal Scots Fusiliers, King's Own Scottish Borderers, Scottish Rifles (Cameronians), Black Watch, Highland Light Infantry, Seaforth Highlanders, Gordon Highlanders, Cameron Highlanders and the Argyll and Sutherland Highlanders, and there are other memorials to the Royal Navy, Flying Services, Royal Marines, Dominions and Colonies, Mercantile Marine, Scotswomen, Indian Army, Nursing Services, Padres, Royal Artillery, Household Cavalry, RAMC, RASC, RE, Scottish Yeomanry, Ordnance, Tank Corps, Veterinary Corps, Machine Gun Corps, London Scottish, South African Scottish, Liverpool Scottish, Tyneside Scottish, Canadian Scottish, and to Scots serving in English, Irish and Welsh Regiments.

There are coats of arms of counties and burghs; memorials to animals such as the one to 'The Tunnellers' Friends' (canaries and mice), and one to carrier pigeons; beautiful stained glass; wonderful stone carvings and statues, both inside and on the exterior; and, in general, so many features and details that no short account can do the subject any justice at all. Of all the books written about the memorial Ian Hay's *Their Name Liveth*, published shortly after the opening ceremony, is perhaps the best-known. The memorial is open to the public, and a visit is necessary for the scale, atmosphere and grandeur of the building to be fully appreciated.

About 200 artists and craftsmen contributed to the memorial and of these Alice Meredith-Williams modelled the figure of St. Michael in the shrine, Morris and Alice Meredith-Williams designed and modelled the bronze frieze in the shrine, Douglas Strachan was responsible for the stained-glass and Alex Carrick for the bronze panels to the Artillery and Engineers, and for the exterior figures of Justice and Courage.

The Prince of Wales formally opened the memorial on 14 July 1927. Colour parties, to the music of *Scots Wha Hae*, placed their colours within the building and then the Prince, in the uniform of the Royal Scots

174

Fusiliers, of which he was Colonel-in-Chief, received the Rolls of Honour and placed them inside the casket. Each Roll was carried by an eminent personality, Field Marshal Earl Haig, for example, carrying the K.O.S.B. Roll, and while this ceremony took place the pipe lament *The Flowers of the Forest* was played.

The Rolls of the Royal Navy, Air Force and Scots Greys were held back to be placed in position by King George V, who arrived with the Queen and Princess Mary, as the first visitor to the memorial, shortly after the opening ceremony by the Prince of Wales and the dedication by the Moderator of the General Assembly of the Church of Scotland, Dr. Norman Maclean.

As *The Scotsman* of the 15 July 1927 put it, 'Scotland, in the presence of the King and Queen, and through the lips of the heir to the throne, paid honour yesterday to her Glorious Dead'.

There is now, on the wall of the Hall of Honour, a bronze plaque with the inscription,

OPENED IN 1927 BY H.R.H. THE PRINCE OF WALES AS A MEMORIAL TO THOSE FROM SCOTLAND WHO DIED IN THE GREAT WAR, THIS IS NOW A SHRINE TO THE MEMORY OF THE FALLEN IN TWO WORLD WARS AND SINCE 1945.

A scene at the opening of the Scottish National War Memorial.
Photograph courtesy of Francis Caird Inglis

THE CALL
1914
A Tribute
to Men and Women of Scottish Blood and Scots origin
in the United States of
AMERICA
to
SCOTLAND
A People that jeoparded their Lives unto the Death
in the high Places of the Field   JUDGES V.18

IF IT BE LIFE THAT...   ...N CONQUERO...

...E AT LAST STRONG IN MY PRIDE AND...

SCOTTISH-AMERICAN MEMORIAL

The Scottish-American Association was inaugurated on 11 November 1919 under the presidency of Lord Weir, and on the plinth of a bronze statue in Princes Street Gardens, Edinburgh, is the inscription,

THE CALL   1914
A TRIBUTE FROM MEN AND WOMEN OF SCOTTISH BLOOD
AND SYMPATHIES IN THE UNITED STATES OF AMERICA TO
SCOTLAND. A PEOPLE THAT JEOPARDED THEIR LIVES UNTO
THE DEATH IN THE HIGH PLACES OF THE FIELD.
JUDGES V 18.

The memorial was unveiled by the American Ambassador, A.B. Houghton, on 7 September 1927.

The sculptor was R. Tait McKenzie of Philadelphia, the architect was Reginald Fairley of Edinburgh, and the cost of the memorial was £10,000.

McKenzie had already completed war memorial commissions in North America and Cambridge, where his bronze, 'The Home-Coming', formed the Cambridgeshire memorial.

His bronze figure of a kilted Scottish soldier, seated but alert, with a rifle across his knees, is the main feature of the Princes Street memorial. The figure is sitting on his greatcoat with his bonnet in his left hand and with his right hand on the trigger guard of his rifle. On a stone plinth the statue faces Edinburgh Castle while behind it is a 50 foot long wall with a bronze frieze and an inscription. The inscription is a quotation from a poem by Lieutenant E.A. McIntosh, MC, of the Seaforth Highlanders who was killed in 1916,

IF IT IS LIFE THAT WAITS I SHALL LIVE
FOREVER UNCONQUERED, IF DEATH, I SHALL DIE AT LAST,
STRONG IN MY PRIDE AND FREE.

The frieze shows a procession of farm workers, shepherds and industrial workers, the figures changing half-way along into those of soldiers marching behind a pipe band.

The heads of the men in the procession were said to have been modelled by the sculptor on those of men in the King's Own Scottish Borderers.

WELSH NATIONAL WAR MEMORIAL

The Welsh National War Memorial stands in Alexandra Gardens, Cardiff. The idea of such a memorial was first mooted in 1917, but really started to take shape in October 1919 when the *Western Mail* opened a fund to which over £25,000 was soon subscribed.

Architectural assessors were appointed, designs were submitted by selected architects, and in July 1924 that of Mr. J.E. Comper was accepted. After some difficulty over choice of site it was decided in August 1925 that the memorial should be built in a central position in Alexandra Gardens, Cardiff. Messrs. E. Turner & Sons Ltd. were given the contract for the masonry work, Mr W.D. Gough of Oxford was commissioned to execute the carving, Mr A.B. Pegram to execute the sculpture, and Mr. A.B. Burton of Thames Ditton to cast the bronze. Pegram's other work included the Preston War Memorial sculpture and a memorial in Norwich to Edith Cavell.

Work commenced in March 1926 and was completed in the summer of 1928. The unveiling was on 12 June 1928, by the Prince of Wales.

The memorial takes the form of a sunken court containing a central fountain and surrounded by a circular colonnade. As part of the fountain there are the bronze figures of a soldier, sailor and airman, each raising up a laurel wreath to a central and higher figure of a winged Messenger of Victory,

his sword held aloft as if it were a cross. Beneath this figure is the inscription,

REMEMBER HERE IN PEACE THOSE WHO IN TUMULT
OF WAR BY SEA, ON LAND, IN AIR, FOR US AND FOR
THE VICTORY ENDURETH UNTO DEATH.

The inscription on the outside of the frieze reads,

I FEIBION CYMRU A RODDES EU BYWYD DROS EI
GWLAD YN RHYFEL MCMXIV-MCMXVIII.

(To the sons of Wales who gave their lives for
their country in the war of 1914-1918.)

Finally, there are appropriate inscriptions in Welsh by poets William Parry and T. Gwyn Jones over the three porches which lead to the figures of the Soldier, Sailor and Airman. For example, that above the sailor is DROS FOR FE DROES I FARW (Over the sea went he to die).

In addition to this monument the names of the Welsh men and women who fell in the war were recorded by Mr. Graely Hewitt, a noted artist in writing and illumination, in a handsomely bound vellum book deposited in the National Museum and later removed to the Temple of Peace.

Today the monument stands in the middle of beautifully-kept gardens and is a most striking and appropriate memorial. At one time there was a danger that the attractive surrounding trees might be allowed to obscure a perfect view of it, but this problem has been overcome.

Bolton

At the time of the unveiling in July 1928 of the Bolton war memorial, designed by Mr. A.J. Hope, it was regretted that two groups of bronze figures, 'Peace Restraining War' and 'Peace Seeing the Horrors of War' were not at that time ready, and might not be until Armistice Day 1929. It was not in fact until just before Armistice Day 1932 that the bronzes were finally placed in position on the memorial, after considerable complaint and correspondence in the local press. The sculptor, Mr. W. Marsden of South Kensington, whose work can be seen also on the St. Anne's memorial, had apparently been 'waiting for inspiration'.

The bronzes were placed on either side of the original memorial arch containing a bronze cross, which four years earlier, had been unveiled in Victoria Square by Lord Derby, and dedicated by the Bishop of Manchester, Dr Temple. Before the main ceremony, which 10,000 people attended, the Bishop had, in the Hall of Remembrance in the Town Hall, dedicated the Roll of Honour with the names of 3,510 men and women of Bolton who fell in the war.

It was later said at a winding-up meeting of the War Memorial Committee, that 'the Committee had to wait a long time but it was worth while, for the statuary was very beautiful indeed and very expressive' and this certainly is the case.

The accounts produced at the same meeting showed that £10,304 11s 7d had been raised of which the Victoria Square memorial had cost £7,761, the Hall of Remembrance £1,765 and the Roll of Honour £400. After other miscellaneous expenses were met a balance of £28 remained, which it was suggested should be handed over to the Royal Infirmary.

To the various inscriptions on the memorial have been added the dates of 1939–1945. One inscription reads,

OUR BROTHERS DIED TO WIN A BETTER WORLD.
OUR PART MUST BE TO STRIVE FOR TRUTH, GOODWILL
AND PEACE THAT THEIR SELF-SACRIFICE BE NOT IN VAIN.

MERCHANT NAVY

After the First World War a colonnade of Portland stone, designed by Sir Edwin Lutyens was built as a war memorial to the merchant navy dead of 1914–18, in Trinity Gardens, close to the Tower of London, and unveiled by Queen Mary on 12 December 1928.

In the stonework above the columns is inscribed,

1914 – 1918
TO THE GLORY OF GOD AND TO THE HONOUR OF TWELVE
THOUSAND OF THE MERCHANT NAVY AND FISHING FLEETS
WHO HAVE NO GRAVE BUT THE SEA.

In 1955, to the colonnade was added a sunken garden, designed by Sir Edward Maufe with statues by Sir Charles Wheeler, the two men who were responsible for the post-1945 additions to the Royal Navy's memorials.

The garden and statues built in memory of the Second World War dead have a wall engraved,

1939 – 1945
THE TWENTY FOUR THOUSAND OF THE MERCHANT NAVY
AND FISHING FLEETS WHOSE NAMES ARE HONOURED ON
THE WALLS OF THE GARDEN GAVE THEIR LIVES FOR
THEIR COUNTRY AND HAVE NO GRAVE BUT THE SEA.

The engraved wall is between two staircases leading down into the garden and is flanked by two stone columns, in front of each of which is a fine stone statue of a seaman.

At frequent intervals around the garden are seating and further sculptures, and, despite being almost surrounded by traffic, the garden still seems to have a tranquil atmosphere.

Bronze plaques on the inside of the walls surrounding the garden list the names of those lost under the names of their ships, the same convention used to list the dead in the First World War colonnade.

The fact that the fatalities for the later war are double the number of the first demonstrates the different nature of the conflict at sea. Churchill was quoted as saying, 'The only thing that ever really frightened me during the war was the U-Boat peril'.

Photograph courtesy of Messrs. Anderson and McMeekin.

BELFAST

The Belfast War Memorial was unveiled on Armistice Day, 11 November 1929, by Field Marshal Lord Allenby, a former Inniskilling Dragoon, who had joined the famous regiment in 1882 and served in it for twenty years.

The dedicatory prayer was offered by the Bishop of Down and Connor and Dromore, the Right Reverend Dr. Grierson.

The memorial was built in a Garden of Remembrance on the west side of the City Hall, and took the form of a 30 foot high cenotaph with the background of a 25 foot high curved colonnade. It was designed by Sir Alfred Brumwell Thomas, who had some thirty years earlier designed the magnificent Belfast City Hall, and constructed by W.J. Campbell.

Part of the inscription on the monument reads,

THROUGHOUT THE LONG YEARS OF STRUGGLE
WHICH HAVE NOW SO GLORIOUSLY ENDED,
THE MEN OF ULSTER HAVE PROVED HOW
NOBLY THEY FIGHT AND DIE – GEORGE R.

LIVERPOOL

The dedication of Liverpool's war memorial did not take place until Armistice Day 1930, twelve years to the day after the end of the war. By then, as the local British Legion pointed out, Liverpool was practically the only place in the country without a permanent memorial, a temporary wooden cenotaph having been used for many years for Remembrance ceremonies.

Several years of delay had been caused by the Lord Mayor's announcement in November 1920 that he was postponing his appeal in connection with a memorial, 'in view of the amount of unemployment now existing'. It was not until November 1925 that another scheme was initiated, and the following year an open competition to choose a design for the city's memorial attracted entries of 767 drawings and 39 models.

From these the design of Lionel B. Budden, Associate Professor in Architecture at Liverpool University, was chosen.

The design was for a long rectangular monument of Darley Dale stone, altar-like in shape. The site for the memorial was to be the plateau below St. George's Hall, and this determined the shape and material of the design. On the stone were two long bronze friezes with figures in low relief. On the outer face, above a frieze showing figures in mourning, was the inscription,

TO THE MEN OF LIVERPOOL WHO FELL IN THE GREAT WAR

to which has subsequently been added,

AND ALL WHO HAVE FALLEN IN CONFLICT SINCE.

Below the frieze were the words,

AND THE VICTORY THAT DAY WAS TURNED INTO
MOURNING UNTO ALL THE PEOPLE.

The frieze facing the Hall represented marching men of 1914 with the inscription above being,

AS UNKNOWN AND YET WELL KNOWN
AS DYING AND BEHOLD WE LIVE.

and that below reading,

OUT OF THE NORTH PARTS A GREAT COMPANY AND A
MIGHTY ARMY.

The size of the original design was thirty-nine foot long but this was later slightly reduced, and the cost was estimated at £8,000 compared with

Photograph courtesy of *Liverpool Daily Post and Echo Limited*.

UNTO·ALL·THE·PEOPLE

TO·THE·MEN·OF·

AND·THE·VICTORY·THAT·

the stipulated maximum of £10,000. The sculpture was the responsibility of G.H. Tyson Smith, the well-known Liverpool sculptor.

Even after the design had been chosen there was criticism of the scheme. The choice of the site in front of St. George's Hall was felt to reduce the effect of the Hall's architecture, the removal of Disraeli's statue to the steps of the Hall to accommodate the memorial was criticised, and the scale of the memorial was questioned. However, it was pointed out that much of the criticism came from architects who had been unsuccessful in the design competition and gradually the scheme came to be more accepted.

More controversy arose when a decision was made that there should be no religious aspect to the unveiling ceremony, to avoid any division of feeling between the religious communities. Widespread condemnation of this incredible decision resulted in a last minute change, and in the event a dedicatory prayer was offered by the chaplain of the 55th Division, the Reverend J.R. Beresford, and when a wreath was laid by the Catholic Archbishop of Liverpool, Dr Downey, the *De Profundis* was recited. Prayers were also offered by representatives of the Free Church, the Greek Orthodox Church and the Jewish community.

Lord Derby, the Lord Lieutenant of the County, unveiled the memorial which was covered by a vast green cloth to which 12,000 poppies had been sewn by hand, and which also bore a huge Union Jack, and, in scarlet, the word 'Triumph'. For the unveiling an electrical device had been installed requiring only the pressing of a button.

In May 2003 a nearby plaque commemorating Liverpool's part in the Battle of the Atlantic was unveiled by the Lord Mayor, Councillor Jack Spriggs.

Part of the inscription explains,

THE BATTLE LASTED 5 YEARS 8 MONTHS 4 DAYS;
HAD IT BEEN LOST, SO TOO WOULD HAVE BEEN THE WAR
BY THIS MARKER LIVERPOOL'S UNPARALLELED SERVICE
AND SACRIFICE SHALL NOT BE FORGOTTEN.

ROLLS ROYCE

The Rolls Royce factory at Derby made the Merlin engines for the 1939–1945 wartime Spitfire and Lancaster aircraft, and it is fitting that the entrance hall is the site of a particularly fine Second World War memorial.

Above the staircase is a stained-glass window in the centre of which stands the figure of a young RAF fighter pilot in full flying kit, with flying boots, 'Mae West' and with his helmet in his hand. He is standing on the hub of a propeller, the blades of which dominate the lower half of the window, and he is looking down on the roofs of the Derby factory which produced the engines necessary for his survival and victory. Between him and a huge bright sun in the background, is a golden eagle with wings outstretched.

Incorporated in the work are the words,

THIS WINDOW COMMEMORATES THE PILOTS OF
THE ROYAL AIR FORCE WHO, IN THE BATTLE OF BRITAIN,
TURNED THE WORK OF OUR HANDS INTO
THE SALVATION OF OUR COUNTRY.

The window, designed by Hugh Easton, was unveiled by Marshal of the Royal Air Force Lord Tedder on 11 January 1949, and dedicated by the Lord Bishop of Derby.

Each year on the Monday nearest to 15 September, Battle of Britain Day, a service is held in the hall for ex-RAF servicemen. In 2003 part of the recorded speech by Lord Tedder at the unveiling was played.

Unfortunately the closure of the factory is imminent, and a decision has still to be made as to the re-siting of the window.

$\mathscr{S}$T George's Chapel, Biggin Hill

RAF Biggin Hill is now closed, but St. George's Chapel of Remembrance remains as a reminder of perhaps the most famous station of the Battle of Britain.

Biggin Hill squadrons provided cover for the Dunkirk evacuation in May 1940, and, from August to the end of the year, seven squadrons from the airfield were involved in the Battle of Britain, accounting for the destruction of some 600 enemy aircraft. Throughout the war, 1,400 enemy were destroyed by the fifty or so squadrons of the sector.

The foundation stone for the Chapel was laid by Air Chief Marshal Lord Dowding, and the building was dedicated on 10 November 1951 by the Bishop of Rochester. This beautiful Chapel has so many remarkable features, that no short description can possibly do it justice.

The reredos panels have inscribed on them the names of 453 pilots of the fifty-two squadrons of the Biggin Hill sector, plus two Station Commanders, who lost their lives in the war. The names are recorded by squadron and the badge of each squadron appears on the panel. Above the reredos are the battle honours of 'DUNKIRK', 'BATTLE OF BRITAIN', 'DIEPPE', 'PAS DE CALAIS', 'NORMANDY', 'ARNHEM', 'RUHR' and 'RHINE'.

The altar frontal is embroidered with the emblems of the British Isles and the Allied Countries, and a quotation from Psalm 63, '*In the shadow of thy wings will I rejoice*'. The font was presented by the Marshal of the Royal Air Force, Lord Tedder, in 1957, on behalf of the Royal Air Force Association. A Roll of Honour and a Book of Remembrance provide the names of those from Biggin Hill who died in the Battle of Britain, and those who died during the war.

The windows are the most striking aspect of the whole building. Those in the body of the Chapel were made in the studio of Hugh Easton who designed the Battle of Britain memorial window in Westminster Abbey, and were donated variously by companies, or RAF formations, or to commemorate individuals. Alike in basic design, one, for example, has the inscription, 'And some there be who have no memorial', and was given anonymously. Another is to two brothers, Flying Officer Ivo Cuthbert, killed in May 1940, and Major Sydney John Cuthbert, of the Scots Guards,

F/O Gerald Ivo Cuthbert R.A.F. of 601 Squadron killed in action in May 1940. Major Sidney John Cuthbert Scots Guards, his brother, killed in action in July 1944.

All things which are that laughed so bright, extravagantly fallen in the light.

Weep for them! Weep for Youth

I FEAR NO MAN

THE STRONGEST LINK

killed in July 1944. Others were given by Rolls Royce, Vickers Armstrong, Hawker, and by Lloyds.

In St. George's Room the west window depicts St. George, and was installed in 1981 to commemorate the 40th Anniversary of the Battle of Britain. In the top part of this window are the badges of the seven squadrons serving at Biggin Hill during the battle. Another four windows in St. George's Room were installed in 1985 to commemorate the ground services of the RAF, 'Ground Control', 'Rescue Services', 'Aircraft Servicing', and 'Parachute Packing'. In the corner of the 'Ground Control' window are shown three Military Medals, awarded to three WAAF members for bravery during two 1940 attacks on the airfield. All the windows in St. George's Room were designed by Goddard and Gibbs.

There are also, within the Chapel, plaques commemorating Polish and Canadian airmen, a plaque of Delft tiles given in gratitude for the hospitality shown to Dutch airmen, and a low cupboard on a stand, in memory of 100 Norwegian pilots who died whilst serving with RAF Fighter Command. On the doors of the cupboard are the badges of 331 and 332 Squadrons. The altar ornaments are an Australian gift and finally a wooden bench seat was presented in 1962 in memory of the American pilots who gave their lives whilst serving with Fighter Command.

Outside the chapel is a Garden of Remembrance featuring lawns, benches, a sundial, a wisteria-covered arbour, and a rose garden in which small crosses have been placed in individual remembrance.

On either side of the entrance gates are a replica Spitfire and Hurricane.

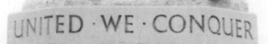

UNITED · WE · CONQUER

IN·MEMORY·OF
THE·OFFICERS·AND
MEN·OF
THE·COMMANDOS
WHO·DIED·IN·THE
SECOND·WORLD·WAR
1939–1945
THIS·COUNTRY·WAS
THEIR·TRAINING
GROUND

OMMANDOS

Queen Elizabeth the Queen Mother unveiled a monument to the 1,700 Commandos who died in the 1939–1945 war, on a hillside site at Spean Bridge, Inverness-shire, on 27 September 1952. The memorial, three, 9 foot tall bronze figures by Scott Sutherland on a stone block plinth, was erected on the hillside overlooking Ben Nevis because the countryside around was the training ground for Commandos during the war.

During the ceremony, Lord Lovat, the wartime Commando leader, made an address to the large crowd, which included many former Commandos, and a lone piper played the lament *Flowers o' the Forest* at the foot of the statue.

A subsequent plaque commemorates the granting of the freedom of Lochaber to the Commando Association on 13 November 1993 and also reads,

FOR THEIR VALOUR IN ACTION THE COMMANDOS EARNED THIRTY-EIGHT BATTLE HONOURS AND MANY AWARDS, INCLUDING EIGHT VICTORIA CROSSES, BUT MANY MADE THE SUPREME SACRIFICE. NO FEWER THAN 1,700 COMMANDO SOLDIERS LOST THEIR LIVES AND OTHERS WERE SERIOUSLY WOUNDED. IT WAS A RECORD THAT PROMPTED WINSTON CHURCHILL TO PAY THE FOLLOWING TRIBUTE TO THE COMMANDOS. 'WE MAY FEEL SURE THAT NOTHING OF WHICH WE HAVE ANY KNOWLEDGE OR RECORD HAS EVER BEEN DONE BY MORTAL MEN, WHICH SURPASSES THEIR FEATS OF ARMS. TRULY WE MAY SAY OF THEM, WHEN SHALL THEIR GLORY FADE'.

ELIZABETH & CHARLES VYNER

Fountains Hall, in Yorkshire, has one of the most touching of memorials to individuals. Inside the Hall, above the entrance staircase, the memorial is to Elizabeth Vyner, WRNS, who died on active service on 3 June 1942 aged eighteen, and to her brother Charles de Grey Vyner, sub-lieutenant in the RNVR, who was reported missing off Rangoon on 2 May 1945 aged nineteen.

The memorial features a stained glass window surrounding a stone cross bearing two wreaths. To the left of the window stands the stone figure of a Wren and to the right the figure of an airman. Each figure is looking upwards towards the cross. On the glass are the words,

WHEN YOU GO HOME TELL THEM OF US AND SAY,
FOR YOUR TOMORROW WE GAVE OUR TODAY.

(the Kohima epitaph), and in stone between the two figures are the words,

FROM THIS THEIR HOME THEY WENT FORTH TO WAR.

This dignified and touching memorial was designed by John, Lord Mottistone and Paul Paget, and executed by sculptor Cecil Thomas and stained-glass artist Hugh Easton. It was unveiled on 9 April 1953 by Queen Elizabeth the Queen Mother, a friend of the Vyner family.

WHEN YOU GO HOME
TELL THEM OF US
AND SAY
FOR YOUR TOMORROW
WE GAVE OUR TODAY

FROM THIS THEIR HOME
THEY WENT FORTH TO WAR

ELIZABETH VYNER · W·R·N·S
DIED ON ACTIVE SERVICE JUNE 3ᴿᴰ 1942
AGED 18 YEARS · ALSO HER BROTHER
CHARLES DE GREY VYNER
SUB LIEUT (A) R · N · V · R
REPORTED MISSING FROM AIR OPERATIONS
OFF RANGOON MAY 2ᴺᴰ 1945 · AGED 19 YEARS

AIR FORCES, RUNNYMEDE

At the beginning of the eighteenth century Alexander Pope wrote, prophetically, 'On Cooper's Hill eternal wreaths shall grow, while lasts the mountain, or while Thames shall flow'.

On 17 October 1953 the Queen unveiled the Air Forces Memorial on Cooper's Hill, Runnymede, to the memory of over 20,000 airmen who were lost in Second World War operations from bases in the United Kingdom, and North and Western Europe, and who have no known graves. The largest group of those commemorated were from the Royal Air Force, with over 15,000 lost. All parts of the Commonwealth were represented, as were many countries whose airmen flew from Britain after their own lands had been occupied. During the war over 116,000 men and women of Britain and the Commonwealth's Air Forces gave their lives, and almost a third have no known graves. As well as those at Runnymede, other names are similarly recorded throughout the world.

To quote the Queen's speech on the occasion of the unveiling, 'As only free men can, they knew the value of that for which they fought, and that the price was worth paying'.

The memorial of Portland stone and with Westmorland green slate roof, is situated in grounds of some six acres planted with trees, magnolias, azaleas and rhododendrons, and looks out over the water meadows where Magna Carta, enshrining man's basic freedoms, was sealed in 1215.

The design, by Sir Edward Maufe, is a cloister with curved wings, surmounted by a tower containing a vaulted shrine, and with a triple arched entrance. In front of the shrine is a Stone of Remembrance and above it are three stone figures by Vernon Hill representing 'Justice', 'Victory' and 'Courage'. An Astral Crown of blue and gold surmounts the tower. The names of the dead are recorded on the walls of the cloister with narrow windows lighting the stone, giving the impression of partially opened books. Arms of the Commonwealth decorate the cloister ceilings.

Engraved on the great north window of the shrine are words from Psalm 139, the 'Airman's Psalm',

> If I climb up into Heaven, Thou art there.
> If I go to Hell, Thou art there also.
> If I take the wings of the morning
> And remain in the uttermost parts of the sea,
> Even there also shall Thy hand lead me;
> And Thy right hand shall hold me.

The site, the grounds, and the buildings themselves combine to make this one of the most atmospheric of all war memorials.

Admiral Ramsay

Admiral Sir Bertram Ramsay commanded the seaborne forces both at Dunkirk in 1940 and at Normandy in 1944. In 1945, with victory secured, he died when the Hudson aircraft carrying him and four of his staff, crashed on take-off, killing all on board.

In Portsmouth Cathedral, below the D-Day Commemoration Window, are two windows by Edwards and Powell, installed in 1956, as a memorial to Ramsay, with the joint inscription,

> 'In memory of Admiral Sir Bertram Ramsay killed in action 1945 who commanded the seaborne forces at Dunkirk 1940 and Normandy 1944. Here are remembered also those under his command who were killed during these operations.'

The left-hand window features St. Nicholas, patron saint of sailors, the shields of Dover and Dunkirk, the black eagle of the Ramsays, and a scene of soldiers being rescued from the sea by a small boat, with the Dunkirk beaches in the background.

The right-hand window depicts St. George, patron saint of soldiers, the arms of the Diocese of Portsmouth and the leopards of Normandy, the shoulder flash of the Supreme Headquarters Allied Expeditionary Force, and a scene of troops landing on the Normandy beaches with the Channel and assault craft behind them.

A nettle in the first window and a flower in the second refer to Hotspur's speech in Shakespeare's *Henry IV* part I, '*out of this nettle, danger, we pluck this flower, safety*'.

In memory of ADMIRAL
SIR BERTRAM RAMSAY
killed in action 1945 who
commanded the seaborne
forces at Dunkirk 1940

and Normandy 1944
here are remembered
also those under his
command who were killed
during these operations

WINSTON CHURCHILL

The memorial to Winston Churchill in Parliament Square, London, a bronze statue on a stone plinth and facing Big Ben, is the work of Ivor Robert-Jones, whose bronzes of Field Marshals Alanbrooke and Slim are in nearby Whitehall, outside the Ministry of Defence. It was unveiled by the Queen in 1973, eight years after Churchill's death.

The sculptor was selected after a competition and the site facing the Houses of Parliament was the choice of Churchill himself, but his widow was unhappy with the completed work and other criticism followed.

The 12 foot bulk of Robert-Jones' Churchill is certainly uncompromising and has been said to make all other statues in the square look like matchstick men. Nevertheless, it surely captures the spirit and will of its subject, dressed in a greatcoat and leaning on a walking stick and with an expression of self-confidence and determination.

INTERNATIONAL BRIGADE

The International Brigade Memorial in Jubilee Gardens, London, next to the London Eye and across the Thames from the Houses of Parliament, was unveiled on 5 October 1985 by Michael Foot, former leader of the Labour Party.

Amongst the speakers were Michael Foot himself, Tony Banks the Chairman of the Greater London Council, and Norman Willis, General Secretary of the TUC.

The inscription on the front of the plinth reads,

INTERNATIONAL BRIGADE
IN HONOUR OF OVER 2,100 MEN AND WOMEN
VOLUNTEERS WHO LEFT THESE SHORES TO FIGHT SIDE BY
SIDE WITH THE SPANISH PEOPLE IN THEIR HEROIC
STRUGGLE AGAINST FASCISM 1936-1939.

MANY WERE WOUNDED AND MAIMED. 526 WERE KILLED
THEIR EXAMPLE INSPIRED THE WORLD.

On one side are Byron's lines,

YET FREEDOM! YET THY BANNER,
TORN, BUT FLYING, STREAMS
LIKE THE THUNDER-STORM
AGAINST THE WIND.

and on the other, paraphrasing C. Day Lewis,

THEY WENT BECAUSE THEIR OPEN EYES
COULD SEE NO OTHER WAY.

The powerful bronze sculpture by Ian Walters stands, with its plinth, $4\frac{1}{2}$ metres high. Four figures support a wounded central figure with mutilated right arm. The free hands of the supporting four are stretched above them, two with open palms as if to fend off further attack, and two with clenched fists in a gesture of defiance.

Each year there is a pilgrimage of remembrance to the memorial.

INTERNATIONAL
BRIGADE

IN HONOUR OF OVER 2100 MEN &
WOMEN VOLUNTEERS WHO LEFT
THESE SHORES TO FIGHT SIDE
BY SIDE WITH THE SPANISH PEOPLE
IN THEIR HEROIC STRUGGLE
AGAINST FASCISM 1936 - 1939
MANY WERE WOUNDED AND
MAIMED 526 WERE KILLED
THEIR EXAMPLE INSPIRED
THE WORLD

"THEY WENT BECAUSE THEIR
OPEN EYES
COULD SEE NO OTHER WAY"

HE DAMBUSTERS

The memorial to 617 Squadron RAF, the 'Dambusters' was dedicated on 17 May 1987 in Royal Square Gardens, Woodhall Spa, the squadron having been based at Woodhall after originally being at Scampton. The architect for this imaginative work was K. Stevens ARIBA and it stands in a well-kept pretty garden with a backing screen of trees.

The York-stone memorial, some ten foot high, represents a dam, and in the centre a grey-green section, sloping outwards, represents the torrent of released water. On this section is the squadron badge, again depicting a shattered dam, and the motto 'Apres moi, le deluge'. Also here are the squadron battle honours, starting with 'The Dams 1943'. To each side of this section are three green slate panels with the names of the 204 aircrew who lost their lives in the war. Above are the words,

THEY DIED FOR YOUR FREEDOM

On the night of 16-17 May 1943, nineteen Lancasters of 617 Squadron attacked the Ruhr Dams at low level. In carrying out the attacks using the bouncing bombs specially designed by Barnes Wallis, the Squadron led by Wing Commander Guy Gibson lost eight of the nineteen aircraft and although the Mohne and Eder dams were breached, real damage to the German war effort was not significant or lasting. The psychological importance of the raid was never in doubt, however. Gibson, aged twenty-four, already the holder of a DSO and two DFCs, was awarded the VC but died the following year on a Mosquito sortie. The extremely high percentage loss of aircraft in the attack did not encourage similar raids. Max Hastings, author of *Bomber Command* quotes Sir Arthur Harris as saying, many years later, 'Any operation deserving of the Victoria Cross, by its nature, is unfit to be repeated at regular intervals'.

International Air Monument

Close to the Armada and Royal Navy memorials on Plymouth Hoe, the Royal Air Force International Air Monument was unveiled on 3 September 1989, by Air Marshal Sir John Curtiss. The ceremony marked the culmination of nine years of work by Jim Davis, an ex air gunner, of Plymouth. He had the vision and energy to instigate the project and to bring it to fruition, and was rewarded with the city's Award for Service to the Community.

The unveiling took place before a crowd of some 20,000 people and representatives of seventeen countries, and in the subsequent fly past were a Spitfire and a Hurricane of the RAF Battle of Britain Memorial Flight.

The main feature of the 18 foot high memorial is the bronze figure by Pamela Taylor of the 'Unknown Airman' in flying kit, on a column of polished Cornish granite. Panels of black polished marble on the column carry, in gold lettering, tributes to those commemorated, and information about the part played by the Air Force in the Second World War. The top panel has the wording, under a gilt eagle,

ROYAL AIR FORCE COMMONWEALTH AND
ALLIED AIR FORCES 1939-1945.

On the bottom plaque is the epitaph,

THEY FLEW BY DAY AND NIGHT AND GAVE THEIR LIVES TO
KEEP FOREVER BRIGHT THAT PRECIOUS LIGHT FREEDOM.

Elsewhere are tributes to the RAF leaders Bennett, Dowding, Harris, Portal, Slessor and Tedder, and to Arnold, Eaker, and Spaatz of the US Air Force. Also honoured are 107,000 members of the RAF, 84,000 members of the USAF and 42,000 members of the Soviet Air Force. Of the RAF losses it is recorded that Bomber Command lost 58,378, Coastal Command 13,225, Fighter Command 7,436, SEAC 6,182 and the Middle East 13,225. A version of Churchill's famous words is also engraved,

NEVER IN THE FIELD OF HUMAN CONFLICT HAS SO
MUCH BEEN OWED BY SO MANY TO SO FEW.

ROYAL AIR FORCE
COMMONWEALTH & ALLIED AIR FORCES
1939 – 1945

TRIBUTE
TO ALL MEN AND WOMEN OF GREAT BRITAIN
AUSTRALIA, CANADA, INDIA, NEW ZEALAND,
RHODESIA AND SOUTH AFRICA,
BELGIUM, CZECHOSLOVAKIA, DENMARK,
FRANCE, GREECE, THE NETHERLANDS,
NORWAY AND POLAND
THE UNITED STATES OF AMERICA,
THE UNION OF SOVIET SOCIALIST REPUBLICS
& THOSE OF MANY OTHER NATIONS WHO SERVED
IN ALL COMMANDS OF THE ROYAL AIR FORCE,
COMMONWEALTH AND ALLIED AIR FORCES,
DURING THE SECOND WORLD WAR.

THEIR COURAGE SKILL AND DEVOTION TO DUTY
WAS OF THE HIGHEST ORDER.

BY WINNING THE BATTLE OF BRITAIN, THE MEN
AND WOMEN OF FIGHTER AND OTHER COMMANDS
SAVED THIS COUNTRY FROM INVASION IN 1940
"NEVER IN THE FIELDS OF HUMAN CONFLICT HAS SO
MUCH BEEN OWED BY SO MANY TO SO FEW"
CHURCHILL

COASTAL COMMAND PLAYED A VITAL ROLE IN
KEEPING THE SEA LANES OPEN.

THE COMMANDS IN THE MIDDLE EAST, AFRICA AND
THE FAR EAST MADE GREAT CONTRIBUTIONS
TOWARDS FINAL VICTORY.

FROM THE OUTBREAK OF WAR THE BOMBER
OFFENSIVE STEADILY INCREASED AND AFTER THE
FORMATION OF THE PATHFINDER GROUP IN 1942
VERY SEVERE DAMAGE WAS INFLICTED ON THE
ENEMY BY THE CONSTANT NIGHT AND DAY
OPERATIONS CARRIED OUT BY BOMBER COMMAND
AND THE UNITED STATES AIR FORCES.

CONTROL OF THE SKIES OVER EUROPE IN 1944
WAS A VITAL FACTOR TO THE SUCCESS OF THE
NORMANDY LANDINGS. THE COMBINED EFFORTS OF
TACTICAL AND BOMBER COMMANDS AND
THE UNITED STATES AIR FORCE THEN SPEARHEADED
THE ALLIED ADVANCE ACROSS EUROPE.

THE INSPIRED LEADERSHIP OF BENNETT, DOWDING,
HARRIS, PORTAL, SLESSOR AND TEDDER OF THE
ROYAL AIR FORCE AND ARNOLD, EAKER & SPAATZ
OF THE UNITED STATES AIR FORCE PAVED THE WAY
TO VICTORY IN 1945.

"NOW AT LAST THE BOMBER COMMANDS HAVE WON
THE AIR BATTLE OF EUROPE OPENING THE PATH
FOR VICTORY AND FREEDOM FOR THE ENSLAVED
COUNTRIES OF EUROPE."
CHURCHILL 1945.

HONOUR
107,000 MEMBERS OF THE ROYAL AIR FORCE,
54,000 MEMBERS OF THE UNITED STATES AIR FORCE,
42,200 MEMBERS OF THE SOVIET AIR FORCE,
WHO MADE THE ULTIMATE SACRIFICE.

THEY FLEW BY DAY AND NIGHT
AND GAVE THEIR LIVES TO KEEP FOREVER BRIGHT
THAT PRECIOUS LIGHT,
FREEDOM.

IREFIGHTERS

In the floor of St Paul's Cathedral is a large inlaid stone plaque with the words,

REMEMBER MEN AND WOMEN OF SAINT PAUL'S WATCH
WHO BY THE GRACE OF GOD SAVED THIS CATHEDRAL
FROM DESTRUCTION IN WAR 1939 – 1945.

Fittingly, outside the cathedral but still very close to it, another memorial was unveiled by the Queen Mother, on 4 May 1991, to the firefighters who gave their lives during the 'Blitz' and the Second World War.

Called 'Heroes with grimy faces' by Churchill, some one thousand firemen and women are commemorated on this national monument, their names appearing on bronze tablets on the base. One tablet, with reliefs of women in uniform, lists the names of twenty-three women who died.

The main feature of the memorial is a dramatic group of three firemen by sculptor John W. Mills. Two of the figures are directing a hose-pipe while the third, looking to the rear, points to the fire and gestures for further help.

In recent years the memorial has been moved from its original position to another close by, and an additional base has been added with a plaque reading,

THIS MEMORIAL WAS RE-DEDICATED THE UNITED
KINGDOM FIREFIGHTERS NATIONAL MEMORIAL AND
UNVEILED BY HER ROYAL HIGHNESS THE PRINCESS ROYAL
(PATRON OF THE FIREFIGHTERS MEMORIAL TRUST)
16 SEPTEMBER 2003.

$\mathscr{F}$ALKLANDS ROYAL MARINES

One of the enduring images of the Falklands War was the line of Royal Marines making their way on foot, heavily laden with arms and equipment, across the rough terrain towards Port Stanley, with the Union Jack fluttering above them as they 'yomped'.

Ten years after the war a statue was unveiled with an inscription plaque reading, under the badge of the Royal Marines,

'YOMPER'

THIS STATUE WAS UNVEILED BY
BARONESS THATCHER OF KESTEVEN O.M., P.C., F.R.S.
ON 8 JULY 1992 TO COMMEMORATE ALL
THE ROYAL MARINES AND THOSE WHO SERVED
WITH THEM IN THE SOUTH ATLANTIC
DURING THE FALKLANDS WAR OF 1982.

The statue in question is a formidable figure by Midhurst sculptor Philip Jackson, standing high on a grass bank at the entrance to the Royal Marines Museum, Eastney, Southsea in Hampshire, and looking out across the Solent.

In her speech at the unveiling ceremony Lady Thatcher, prime minister at the time of the war, spoke of 'the freedom and justice we take for granted until it is taken away by a dictator', and compared the Marines fighting against the odds in the Falklands with the RAF pilots doing the same in the Battle of Britain.

Amongst those introduced to Lady Thatcher was Peter Robinson who appeared in the photograph which inspired the idea of the 'Yomper'.

BATTLE OF BRITAIN

On 9 July, 1993, Queen Elizabeth the Queen Mother unveiled a memorial to those who flew in the Battle of Britain, at a site on top of the white cliffs at Capel-le-Ferne, near Dover. Harry Gray's stone statue of a pilot, seated on a base bearing the crests of almost seventy squadrons involved in the battle, was covered by a Second World War parachute which was lifted off by RAF officers, watched by the 92 year old Queen Mother. Blustering wind and rain prevented an air display of Spitfire, Hurricane and Blenheim aircraft but did not prevent 130 veterans of the 1940 battle, and several thousand others, from attending the ceremony.

The statue of the young fighter pilot looking out to sea forms the centre-piece of an area some 100 yards across and featuring the three thirty-eight metre long blades of a propeller cut into the ground, with the statue and base as its hub.

The inspiration for the memorial came from the chairman of the Battle of Britain Memorial Trust, Wing Commander Geoffrey Page, DSO, DFC and bar, who was a twenty-year-old pilot in the summer of 1940. He was badly injured during the battle and severe burns to his hands and face resulted in two years in hospital, but he returned to fly again until his wartime career was terminated after further injuries resulting from crash-landing his Spitfire at Arnhem.

A unit at Queen Victoria Hospital, East Grinstead, headed by Sir Archibald McIndoe, specialised in the first modern plastic surgery, and the wartime patients of McIndoe became known as the Guinea-Pig Club.

There is now a Visitors Centre at Capel-le-Ferne and boards in the car park give useful information and background to the battle which lasted from 10 July 1940 until the end of October, and during which some 500 Allied pilots lost their lives before the Luftwaffe accepted defeat.

Nearby there is a flagpole with a brass plaque inscribed,

THIS FLAGPOLE WAS DISMANTLED AT THE TIME
OF THE CLOSURE OF R.A.F. BIGGIN HILL IN KENT IN
OCTOBER 1992. IT STANDS AS A SENTINEL TO THIS
MEMORIAL AND SERVES FOREVER AS A PERPETUAL
LINK WITH ALL FIGHTER STATIONS FROM WHICH R.A.F.
SQUADRONS FLEW IN THE BATTLE OF BRITAIN.

A memorial wall donated by the Beaverbrook Foundation has, carved on it, Winston Churchill's immortal words,

'NEVER IN THE FIELD OF HUMAN CONFLICT WAS SO
MUCH OWED BY SO MANY TO SO FEW.'

FALKLAND ISLANDS MEMORIAL CHAPEL

The Falkland Islands Memorial Chapel at Pangbourne College, in Berkshire, was dedicated by the Bishop of Reading on 18 November 1999 when the bereaved families were greeted in the first service held there.

The official opening by Her Majesty the Queen followed on 9 March 2000, when Lady Thatcher and Admiral Sir John Woodward, who led the British forces in the war, were present.

There is now an Annual Service of Remembrance held on the Saturday nearest to 14 June, marking the date of the cessation of hostilities in 1982, and, with a full time chaplain and college choir to staff the Chapel, there are regular services in term time to which the bereaved are invited.

The Chapel commemorates 255 servicemen and three civilians who died in the war, and their names are carved in alphabetical order in stone within the foyer area. They are also listed, by service with ranks and titles included, in a Book of Remembrance housed in a showcase, also in the foyer. The book was sponsored by the Royal Marines, and the showcase by the Parachute Regiment and Airborne Forces. The author Frederick Forsyth sponsored the stonework carving of the names.

Another unusual commemoration of the dead is on 258 kneelers embroidered with individual names, almost half the kneelers in the Chapel, which, within the ground floor area and the gallery, seats 580.

The design for the beautiful stone and red brick Chapel, which cost £2.3 million, was the work of Crispin Wride Architectural Design Studio in Reading. It was chosen from seventy-three entries in a national competition sponsored by the Royal Fine Art Commission.

It is described as depicting hands cupped in prayer, or safeguarding something precious within, while at the same time reminiscent of the shape of a ship.

Unusual external features are a circular Memorial Garden with rocks, moving water, seating, and trees, plants and grasses indigenous to the Falkland Islands; and, outside the main door, a cairn of stones to which those who wish to remember relatives, friends or colleagues from 1982 are encouraged to add their tribute.

The outstanding internal feature is the wonderful stained glass Memorial Window depicting the Falkland Islands surrounded by the stormy Atlantic Ocean. It is the work of John Clark, who created the Lockerbie Memorial Window, and is in vibrant shades of blue and green.

Also inside is a Memorial Room, an Education Room and the St. Nicholas Side Chapel for personal contemplation.

From the gallery can be viewed the Old Pangbournian Window in memory of 177 Old Boys who died serving in the Second World War. In 1982, forty-five Old Pangbournians served in the Falklands and fourteen won distinctions.

220

TANK CREWS

Millennium year saw the unveiling of many new memorials, amongst them the Tank Crews Memorial, on a corner of Whitehall Court, London, near the Ministry of Defence. This was unveiled on 13 June 2000 by her Majesty Queen Elizabeth II, Colonel-in-Chief of the Royal Tank Regiment.

The bronze group of the work represents the crew of a Second World War Comet tank, and is dedicated to all tank crews from the early machines of the Great War to their modern counterparts.

The sculptor was Vivien Mallock from an original design by the late G.H. Paulin and on the base of the group is the motto,

FROM MUD, THROUGH BLOOD, TO THE GREEN
FIELDS BEYOND.

SHOT AT DAWN

The National Memorial Arboretum (NMA) at Alrewas, Staffordshire, was officially opened on 16 May 2001 by HRH the Duchess of Kent.

A few weeks later the unveiling and dedication of the Shot at Dawn Memorial took place at the NMA on Thursday, 1 June.

Even during the First World War, the question of military executions for cowardice, desertion and less common offences such as mutiny, treason and murder, was debated and the matter raised repeatedly in Parliament.

Judge Anthony Babington, whose book on First World War capital courts martial *For the Sake of Example* was published in 1983, was the first author to be granted access to the court martial records in the Public Record Office as they were 'closed documents' at that time. His book does not give the names of the men executed but refers to them only by their rank and initials.

By the end of the decade PRO files were released giving details of prosecution proceedings, sentencing and so on and the book *Shot at Dawn* by Julian Putkowski and Julian Sykes was able to provide full information.

In recent years a campaign has sought posthumous pardons for the majority of the executed men, and the New Zealand government has granted such pardons to their five executed soldiers. The British Government has for the moment ruled out any retrospective pardons.

The question is clearly a difficult one to determine by generalisation. On the one hand are the arguments that a blanket pardon devalues the memory of those who, though afraid nevertheless overcame their fear and did their duty; that very few men were executed during a war in which millions died; that of 3,080 British soldiers sentenced to death only ten per cent had their sentences confirmed and ninety per cent on examination had their death sentences commuted; that many of those shot had previous convictions and that a number were under a suspended death sentence for a previous offence; and that it is impossible to judge such things in hindsight and particularly after eighty or more years.

On the other hand, even by the standards of the time, there can be genuine reasons for concern that there were clear deficiencies in court procedures where a man could be sentenced to death without medical evidence being presented that he had returned to the front from lengthy treatment for shell shock; that three seventeen-year-olds, who had clearly concealed their true age in order to fight for their country, could be executed; that men were sometimes undefended at their trial and sometimes

Jack Davis and Fred Bundy at the Unveiling Ceremony.

Photograph courtesy of Sue Elliott.

no proper attempt was made to find character witnesses; and that the German army, twice the size of the British army, had only a handful of men executed (one estimate is forty-eight).

The Shot at Dawn memorial itself, which was funded mainly by individual donations, has at its centre a sculpture created by Andy DeComyn, a Birmingham-based sculptor who has other works in place in the NMA. The sculpture has a concrete core with rendering and is $8^1/_2$ foot tall. It is based on the figure of Pte. Herbert Burden who, at sixteen, added two years to his age in order to enlist in the Northumberland Fusiliers. At seventeen, he deserted at Ypres after his unit suffered huge losses. He was court martialled on 2 July 1915 and executed on 21 July. Despite his age, he was undefended at his trial and, because of his battalion's heavy casualties, no character witnesses could be found at the time of the trial.

The figure has his hands tied behind his back, he is blindfolded and round his neck hangs an aiming-disc centred on his chest. The hands of the sculpture are particularly expressive showing the fear and tension of the moment. In front of the figure are six conifers representing the firing-squad and behind are 306 wooden stakes each with the name, age, regiment, rank and date of death of an executed British and Commonwealth soldier. Those guilty of crimes such as murder are not commemorated.

The actual unveiling of the statue was carried out by 87 year-old Mrs. Gertrude Harris, the daughter of Pte. Harry Farr who was executed for cowardice on 18 October 1916. She was 3 years old at the time and did not learn of the nature of her father's death until she was forty, such was the shame felt by her mother subsequently. Pte. Farr had, in fact, been previously admitted to hospital suffering from shell shock and treated for the next five months before returning to the front, facts which if properly presented at his court martial should surely have saved his life.

Among the large number of people attending the ceremony were two veterans of the First World War, 106 year-old Jack Davis of the Duke of Cornwall's Light Infantry and 100 year-old Fred Bunday of the Royal Navy. Fred had joined the Navy in 1916 and served also in the Second World War as a chief petty officer, finally retiring in 1945 after 28 years service.

Private Herbert Francis Burden
Northumberland Fusiliers
21st July 1915
Aged 17

ANIMALS IN WAR

Perhaps the most interesting and original of recent war memorials was unveiled on Wednesday, 24 November 2004, at Brook Gate, Park Lane, London, by the Princess Royal. The princess is patron of the Animals in War Memorial Fund, of which the board of trustees includes, amongst others, Major General Peter Davies, Brigadier Andrew Parker Bowles and authoress Jilly Cooper.

The purpose of the memorial unveiled is described by one of the inscriptions carved upon its walls,

ANIMALS IN WAR
THIS MONUMENT IS DEDICATED TO ALL THE ANIMALS
THAT SERVED AND DIED ALONGSIDE BRITISH AND ALLIED
FORCES IN WAR AND CAMPAIGNS THROUGHOUT TIME.
THEY HAD NO CHOICE.

Other inscriptions include,

MANY AND VARIOUS ANIMALS WERE EMPLOYED TO
SUPPORT BRITISH AND ALLIED FORCES IN WARS AND
CAMPAIGNS OVER THE CENTURIES AND AS A RESULT
MILLIONS DIED. FROM THE PIGEON TO THE ELEPHANT
THEY ALL PLAYED A VITAL ROLE IN EVERY REGION OF
THE WORLD IN THE CAUSE OF HUMAN FREEDOM. THEIR
CONTRIBUTION MUST NEVER BE FORGOTTEN.

Photograph courtesy of the Animals in War Memorial Fund.

Certainly, a sample of statistics relating to animals' contribution in wartime is both astonishing and horrifying. For example, some eight million horses alone died in the First World War, as well as countless donkeys and mules. An estimated 100,000 pigeons in the Great War and 200,000 in the Second World War were lost. Their chances of survival were put at one in eight. The Indian Army alone in the Burma campaign against the Japanese, used 7,000 mules, often silenced by having their vocal cords cut.

Individual examples of animal heroism include *Rob*, a sheepdog with the SAS, who made more than twenty parachute descents in a series of undercover missions; *Cher Ami*, an American pigeon, which survived the carrying of twelve messages; and pigeon *Mary of Exeter* who returned from one trip savaged by hawks kept by the Germans in the Pas de Calais for the purpose, was later put back in action and completed a further mission with one wing shot away and with three pellets in her body. The most recent recipient of the Dickin Medal, the animal equivalent of the VC, is *Buster*, a springer spaniel sniffer dog used by the army to locate hidden weapons in Iraq.

Only sixty Dickin Medals have ever been awarded and, a few days after the Park Lane unveiling, that awarded to *Commando*, a pigeon used by the Special Operations Executive in 1942, was sold at auction in London for almost £10,000.

The imaginative design for the memorial by Somerset based sculptor David Backhouse consists of a 70 foot Portland stone wall which has a small gap close to one end. Towards this, trudge two heavily laden and resigned gunner mules in bronze, one with lowered head and one with ears back. On the stone wall, carved in relief, are images of the full range of animals used in war, from pigeons to oxen, from elephants to horses, from dogs to camels.

Beyond the gap in the wall, on a grassy hillock, are a bronze horse and dog which seem to symbolise the end of conflict.

The monument, six years in the creation, cost initially £1 million but a further sum of at least £400,000 is required to cover the increased costs relating, for example, to security. On the rear wall of the memorial an acknowledgement of generous public donations is carved, together with a list of principal benefactors, both corporate and individual.

There have in the past been limited British tributes to animals in war, for example that to 'The Tunnellers' Friends' (canaries and mice) and to carrier pigeons in the Scottish National Memorial in Edinburgh, and that to pigeons in Worthing's Beach House Park in the form of a 1949 pool and birdbath, but this latest animal memorial is unique in its scope and scale, in its impact and in its excellence. Its site means that it will demand attention, particularly at night when floodlighting brings out the full effect of the relief carvings, and it has already been said that 'It could be one of London's best loved and most visited memorials'.

INDEX